AN

ESSAY

ON

CRIMES AND PUNISHMENTS,

TRANSLATED FROM THE ITALIAN

OF

CÆSAR BONESANA, MARQUIS BECCARIA.

TO WHICH IS ADDED,

A COMMENTARY,

BY M. D. VOLTAIRE.

TRANSLATED FROM THE FRENCH,

BY EDWARD D. INGRAHAM.

SECOND AMERICAN EDITION.

In rebus quibuscunque difficilioribus non expectandum, ut qui simul, et serat, et metat, sed præparatione opus est, et per gradus maturescant.   BACON.

PHILADELPHIA:
PUBLISHED BY PHILIP H. NICKLIN, NO. 175, CHESNUT ST.

1819.

A. Walker, Printer, 24, Arch St.

District of Pennsylvania, to wit:

※※※※
※Seal.※
※※※※
BE it remembered, that on the thirtieth day of October, in the forty-third year of the Independence of the United States of America, A. D. 1818. *Philip H. Nicklin,* of the said District, has deposited in this office the title of a Book, the right whereof he claims as proprietor, in the words following, to wit:

An Essay on Crimes and Punishments, translated from the Italian of Cæsar Bonesana, Marquis Beccaria. To which is added, a Commentary by M. D. Voltaire. Translated from the French, by Edward D. Ingraham. Second American Edition. In rebus quibusque difficilioribus non expectandum, ut quis simul, et serat, et metat, sed præparatione opus est, et per gradus maturescant.   *Bacon.*

In conformity to the act of Congress of the United States, entitled "An Act for the encouragement of learning, by securing the copies of Maps, Charts and Books, to the authors and proprietors of such copies, during the times therein mentioned;" and also to the act entitled an act "Supplementary to an act entitled, "An Act for the encouragement of learning, by securing the copies of Maps, Charts and Books, to the authors and proprietors of such copies, during the times therein mentioned," and extending the benefits thereof to the arts of Designing, Engraving, and Etching Historical and other Prints.

                 D. CALDWELL,
            Clerk of the District of Pennsylvania.

Publishing Statement:

This important reprint was made from an old and scarce book.

Therefore, it may have defects such as missing pages, erroneous pagination, blurred pages, missing text, poor pictures, markings, marginalia and other issues beyond our control.

Because this is such an important and rare work, we believe it is best to reproduce this book regardless of its original condition.

Thank you for your understanding and enjoy this unique book!

PREFACE

BY THE TRANSLATOR,

OF

M. D. VOLTAIRE'S COMMENTARY.

WHO the author of the translation of M. de Voltaire's commentary upon the Marquis Beccaria's Essay on Crimes and Punishments was, I have never been able to ascertain, but it has always been a matter of regret to me, that it should have been suffered, by its appearance in print, to derogate from the reputation of the original. It appears indeed, at the first view, to be a studied attempt to burlesque the style and misrepresent the sense of that celebrated writer. These circumstances induce me, upon the publication of a new edition of the Essay, to offer a new translation, with the hope that, though it be impossible to transfer to another language the spirit that characterises the style of the original, I might render M. de Voltaire intelligible to the American reader. That this was not the case heretofore, I need only appeal to those who have had the patience to read the version annexed to the first American edition of the Essay on Crimes and Punishments. The reasons are sufficiently obvious; the translator appears to have been imperfectly acquainted with the French language, and totally unacquainted with English or French law terms and proceedings, a knowledge of which is absolutely necessary in order to avoid gross errors in translating a work, in which legal phrases so frequently occur. Proper names also, which the French generally alter to suit their own convenience, appear to have caused him considerable embarrassment: *Mark Antonin* being rendered Mark Anthony, instead of Marcus Antonius; and Madame Brinvilliers, is, from the same cause, metamorphosed into a man. For some reason also all the notes and references by M. de Voltaire are omitted. It may at the same time, not be improper to remark, that the translation being a literal one, the style is uncouth to a degree of barbarism, in consequence of the gallicisms with which it abounds. Let it not be supposed, however, from my strictures upon another, that I am anxious to attract attention to my own work, or to deprecate criticism. Whatever pretensions I may have to notice, are founded upon the belief that I have spared no pains to fulfil the first duty of a translator—a faithful adherence to the sense of my author, at the same time that I have endeavoured to do M. de Voltaire the justice to make him

PREFACE

speak English. How far I have succeeded in my object, is not for me to judge; nor shall I offer any apology for an attempt to render more intelligible any subject connected with the study or improvement of law; convinced, that to make any exertion with that view, is to fulfil one of the first duties which every man owes to his profession.

Philadelphia, September 19, 1819.

CONTENTS.

CHAP.		PAGE
	INTRODUCTION	10
I.	Of the origin of punishments	15
II.	Of the right to punish	17
III.	Consequences of the foregoing principles	20
IV.	Of the interpretation of laws	22
V.	Of the obscurity of laws	26
VI.	Of the proportion between crimes and punishments	28
VII.	Of estimating the degree of crimes	33
VIII.	Of the division of crimes	35
IX.	Of honour	39
X.	Of duelling	42
XI.	Of crimes which disturb the public tranquillity	44
XII.	Of the intent of punishments	47
XIII.	Of the credibility of witnesses	48
XIV.	Of evidence and the proofs of a crime, and of the form of judgment	52
XV.	Of secret accusations	56
XVI.	Of torture	59
XVII.	Of pecuniary punishments	69
XVIII.	Of oaths	72
XIX.	Of the advantage of immediate punishment	74
XX.	Of acts of violence	78
XXI.	Of the punishment of the nobles	79
XXII.	Of robbery	81
XXIII.	Of infamy, considered as a punishment	83
XXIV.	Of idleness	85
XXV.	Of banishment and confiscation	86
XXVI.	Of the spirit of family in states	88

CONTENTS.

CHAP.		PAGE
XXVII.	Of the mildness of punishments	93
XXVIII.	Of the punishment of death	97
XXIX.	Of imprisonment	109
XXX.	Of prosecution and prescription	112
XXXI.	Of crimes of difficult proof	116
XXXII.	Of suicide	122
XXXIII.	Of smuggling	127
XXXIV.	Of bankrupts	130
XXXV.	Of sanctuaries	134
XXXVI.	Of rewards for apprehending or killing criminals	136
XXXVII.	Of attempts, accomplices and pardon	138
XXXVIII.	Of suggestive interrogations	141
XXXIX.	Of a particular kind of crimes	143
XL.	Of false ideas of utility	145
XLI.	Of the means of preventing crimes	148
XLII.	Of the sciences	151
XLIII.	Of magistrates	155
XLIV.	Of rewards	156
XLV.	Of education	ib.
XLVI.	Of pardons	158
XLVII.	Conclusion	160

A COMMENTARY ON THE BOOK OF CRIMES AND PUNISHMENTS.

CHAP.		PAGE
I.	The Circumstances that occasioned this commentary	161
II.	Of Punishments	164
III.	Of the punishment of heretics	166
IV.	Of the exterpation of heresies	170
V.	Of Blasphemy and profanation	174
VI.	Of the indulgence of the Romans in matters of religion	180

CONTENTS.

CHAP.		PAGE
VII.	Of the crime of unlawful preaching. Story of Anthony	183
VIII.	The story of Simon Morin	187
IX.	Of witches	190
X.	Of capital punishment	193
XI.	Of the execution of sentences	196
XII.	Of torture	198
XIII.	Of certain sanguinary tribunals	200
XIV.	Of the difference between political and natural laws	203
XV.	Of the crime of high treason. Of Titus Oates, and of the death of Augustin de Thou	206
XVI.	Of the revealing of crimes (before commission) by religious confession	212
XVII.	Of counterfeiting money	217
XVIII.	Of domestic theft	218
XIX.	Of suicide	219
XX.	Of a certain species of mutilation	222
XXI.	Of the confiscation consequent upon all the crimes which have been mentioned	224
XXII.	Of criminal proceedings, and of some other forms of procedure	229
XXIII.	The idea of a reform suggested	238

B

INTRODUCTION.

IN every human society, there is an effort continually tending to confer on one part the height of power and happiness, and to reduce the other to the extreme of weakness and misery. The intent of good laws is to oppose this effort, and to diffuse their influence universally and equally. But men generally abandoned the care of their most important concerns to the uncertain prudence and discretion of those whose interest it is to reject the best and wisest institutions; and it is not till they have been led into a thousand mistakes in matters the most essential to their lives and liberties, and are weary of suffering, that they can be induced to apply a remedy to the evils with which they are oppressed. It is then they begin to conceive and acknowledge the most palpable truths, which, from their very simplicity, commonly escape vulgar minds, incapable of analysing objects, accustomed to receive impressions without distinction, and to be determined rather by the opinions of others than by the result of their own examination.

If we look into history we shall find that laws, which are, or ought to be, conventions between men in a state of freedom, have been, for the most part the work of the passions of a few, or the consequences of a fortuitous or temporary necessity; not dictated by a cool examiner of human nature, who knew how to collect in one point the actions of a multitude, and had this only end in view, *the greatest happiness of the greatest number.* Happy are those few nations who have not waited till the slow succession of human vicissitudes should, from the extremity of evil, produce a transition to good; but by prudent laws have facilitated the progress from one to the other! And how great are the obligations due from mankind to that philosopher, who, from the obscurity of his closet, had the courage to scatter among the multitude the seeds of useful truths, so long unfruitful!

The art of printing has diffused the knowledge of those philosophical truths, by which the relations between sovereigns and their subjects, and between nations are discovered. By this knowledge commerce is animated, and there has sprung up a spirit of emulation and industry, worthy of rational beings. These are the produce of this enlightened age; but the cruelty of punishments, and the irregularity of proceedings in criminal cases, so principal a part of the legislation, and so much neglected throughout Europe, has hardly ever been called in question. Errors, accumulated through many centuries, have never yet been exposed by ascending to general principles; nor has the force of acknowledged truths been ever opposed to the unbounded licentiousness of ill-directed power, which has continually produced so many authorised examples of the most unfeeling barbarity. Surely, the groans of the weak, sacrificed to the cruel ignorance and indolence of the powerful, the barbarous torments lavished, and multiplied with useless severity, for crimes either not proved, or in their nature impossible, the filth and horrors of a prison, increased by the most cruel tormentor of the miserable, uncertainty, ought to have roused the attention of those whose business is to direct the opinions of mankind.

The immortal Montesquieu has but slightly touched on this subject. Truth, which is eternally the same, has obliged me to follow the steps of that great man; but the studious part of mankind, for whom I write, will easily distinguish the superstructure from the foundation. I shall be happy if, with him, I can obtain the secret thanks of the obscure and peaceful disciples of reason and philosophy, and excite that tender emotion in which sensible minds sympathise with him who pleads the cause of humanity.

AN ESSAY ON CRIMES AND PUNISHMENTS.

CHAP. I.

Of the Origin of Punishments.

LAWS are the conditions under which men, naturally independent, united themselves in society. Weary of living in a continual state of war, and of enjoying a liberty, which became of little value, from the uncertainty of its duration, they sacrificed one part of it, to enjoy the rest in peace and security. The sum of all these portions of the liberty of each individual constituted the sovereignty of a nation and was deposited in the hands of the sovereign, as the lawful administrator. But it was not sufficient only to establish this deposit; it was also necessary to defend it from the usurpation of each individual, who will always endeavour to take away from the mass, not only his own portion, but to encroach on that of others. Some motives therefore, that strike the senses were necessary to prevent the despotism of each individual from plunging society into its former chaos. Such motives are the punishments established against the infractors of the laws. I say that motives of this kind are necessary; because experience shows, that the multitude adopt no established principle of conduct; and because society is prevented from approaching to that dissolution, (to which, as well as all other parts of the physical and moral world, it naturally tends,) only by motives that are the immediate objects of sense, and which being continually presented to the mind, are sufficient to counterbalance the effects of the passions of the individual which oppose the general good. Neither the power of eloquence nor the sublimest truths are sufficient to restrain, for any length of time, those passions which are excited by the lively impressions of present objects.

CHAP. II.

Of the Right to punish.

EVERY punishment which does not arise from absolute necessity, says the great Montesquieu, is tyrannical. A proposition which may be made more general thus: every act of authority of one man over another, for which there is not an absolute necessity, is tyrannical. It is upon this then that the sovereign's right to punish crimes is founded; that is, upon the necessity of defending the public liberty, entrusted to his care, from the usurpation of individuals; and punishments are just in proportion, as the liberty, preserved by the sovereign, is sacred and valuable.

Let us consult the human heart, and there we shall find the foundation of the sovereign's right to punish; for no advantage in moral policy can be lasting which is not founded on the indelible sentiments of the heart of man. Whatever law deviates from this principle will always meet with a resistance which will destroy it in the end; for the smallest force continually applied will overcome the most violent motion communicated to bodies.

No man ever gave up his liberty merely for the good of the public. Such a chimera exists only in romances. Every individual wishes, if possible, to be exempt from the compacts that bind the rest of mankind.

The multiplication of mankind, though slow, being too great, for the means which the earth, in its natural state, offered to satisfy necessities which every day became more numerous, obliged men to separate again, and form new societies. These naturally opposed the first, and a state of war was transferred from individuals to nations.

Thus it was necessity that forced men to give up a part of their liberty. It is certain, then, that every individual would choose to put into the public stock the smallest portion possible, as much only as was sufficient to engage others to defend it. The aggregate of these, the smallest portions possible, forms the right of punishing; all that extends beyond this, is abuse, not justice.

Observe that by *justice* I understand nothing more than that bond which is necessary to keep the interest of individuals united, without which men would return to their original state of barbarity. All punishments which exceed the necessity of preserving this bond are in their nature unjust. We should be cautious how we associate with the word *justice* an idea of any thing real, such as a physical power, or a being that actually exists. I do not, by any means, speak of the justice of God, which is of another kind, and refers immediately to rewards and punishments in a life to come.

CHAP. III.

Consequences of the foregoing Principles.

THE laws only can determine the punishment of crimes; and the authority of making penal laws can only reside with the legislator, who represents the whole society united by the social compact. No magistrate then, (as he is one of the society,) can, with justice, inflict on any other member of the same society punishment that is not ordained by the laws. But as a punishment, increased beyond the degree fixed by the law, is the just punishment with the addition of another, it follows that no magistrate, even under a pretence of zeal, or the public good, should increase the punishment already determined by the laws.

If every individual be bound to society, society is equally bound to him, by a contract which, from its nature equally binds both parties. This obligation, which descends from the throne to the cottage, and equally binds the highest and lowest of mankind, signifies nothing more than that it is the interest of all, that conventions, which are useful to the greatest number, should be punctually observed. The violation of this compact by any individual is an introduction to anarchy.

The sovereign, who represents the society itself, can only make general laws to bind the members; but it belongs not to him to judge whether any individual has violated the social compact, or incurred the punishment in consequence. For in this case there are two parties, one represented by the sovereign, who insists upon the violation of the contract, and the other is the person accused, who denies it. It is necessary then that there should be a third person to decide this contest; that is to say, a judge, or magistrate; from whose determination there should be no appeal; and this determination should consist of a simple affirmation or negation of fact.

If it can only be proved, that the severity of punishments, though not immediately contrary to the public good, or to the end for which they were intended, viz. to prevent crimes, be useless, then such severity would be contrary to those beneficent virtues, which are the consequence of enlightened reason, which instructs the sovereign to wish rather to govern men in a state of freedom and happiness than of slavery. It would also be contrary to justice and the social compact.

CHAP. IV.

Of the Interpretation of Laws.

JUDGES, in criminal cases, have no right to interpret the penal laws, because they are not legislators. They have not received the laws from our ancestors as a domestic tradition, or as the will of a testator, which his heirs and executors are to obey; but they receive them from a society actually existing, or from the sovereign, its representative. Even the authority of the laws is not founded on any pretended obligation, or ancient convention; which must be null, as it cannot bind those who did not exist at the time of its institution; and unjust, as it would reduce men in the ages following, to a herd of brutes, without any power of judging or acting. The laws receive their force and authority from an oath of fidelity, either tacit or expressed, which living subjects have sworn to their sovereign, in order to restrain the intestine fermentation of the private interest of individuals. From hence springs their true and natural authority. Who then is their lawful interpreter? The sovereign, that is, the representative of society, and not the judge, whose office is only to examine if a man have or have not committed an action contrary to the laws.

In every criminal cause the judge should reason syllogistically. The *major* should be the general law; the *minor*, the conformity of the action, or its opposition to the laws; the *conclusion*, liberty, or punishment. If the judge be obliged by the imperfection of the laws, or chooses to make any other or more syllogisms than this, it will be an introduction to uncertainty.

There is nothing more dangerous than the common axiom, *the spirit of the laws is to be considered.* To adopt it is to give way to the torrent of opinions. This may seem a paradox to vulgar minds, which are more strongly affected by the smallest disorder before their eyes, than by the most pernicious though remote consequences produced by one false principle adopted by a nation.

Our knowledge is in proportion to the number of our ideas. The more complex these are, the greater is the variety of positions in which they may be considered. Every man hath his own particular point of view, and, at different times, sees the same objects in very different lights. The spirit of the laws will then be the result of the good or bad logic of the judge; and this will depend on his good or bad digestion, on the violence of his passions, on the rank or condition of the accused, or on his connections with the judge, and on all those little circumstances which change the appearance of objects in the fluctuating mind of man. Hence we see the fate of a delinquent changed many times in passing through the different courts of judicature, and his life and liberty victims to the false ideas or ill humour of the judge, who mistakes the vague result of his own confused reasoning for the just interpretation of the laws. We see the same crimes punished in a different manner at different times in the same tribunals, the consequence of not having consulted the constant and invariable voice of the laws, but the erring instability of arbitrary interpretation.

The disorders that may arise from a rigorous observance of the letter of penal laws are not to be compared with those produced by the interpretation of them. The first are temporary inconveniences which will oblige the legislature to correct the letter of the law, the want of preciseness and uncertainty of which has occasioned these disorders; and this will put a stop to the fatal liberty of explaining, the source of arbitrary and venal declamations. When the code of laws is once fixed, it should be observed in the literal sense, and nothing more is left to the judge than to determine whether an action be or be not conformable to the written law. When the rule of right, which ought to direct the actions of the philosopher, as well as the ignorant, is a matter of controversy, not of fact, the people are slaves to the magistrates. The despotism of this multitude of tyrants is more insupportable the less the distance is between the oppressor and the oppressed, more fatal than that of one, for the tyranny of many is not to be shaken off but by having recourse to that of one alone. It is more cruel, as it meets with more opposition, and the cruelty of a tyrant is not in proportion to his strength, but to the obstacles that oppose him.

These are the means by which security of person and property is best obtained, which is just, as it is the purpose of uniting in society; and it is useful as each person may calculate exactly the inconveniences attending every crime. By these means, subjects will acquire a spirit of independence and liberty, however it may appear to those who dare to call the weakness of submitting blindly to their capricious and interested opinions by the sacred name of virtue.

These principles will displease those who have made it a rule with themselves to transmit to their inferiors the tyranny they suffer from their superiors. I should have every thing to fear if tyrants were to read my book; but tyrants never read.

CHAP. V

Of the Obscurity of Laws.

IF the power of interpreting laws be an evil, obscurity in them must be another, as the former is the consequence of the latter. This evil will be still greater if the laws be written in a language unknown to the people; who, being ignorant of the consequences of their own actions, become necessarily dependent on a few, who are interpreters of the laws, which, instead of being public and general, are thus rendered private and particular. What must we think of mankind when we reflect, that such is the established custom of the greatest part of our polished and enlightened Europe? Crimes will be less frequent in proportion as the code of laws is more universally read and understood; for there is no doubt but that the eloquence of the passions is greatly assisted by the ignorance and uncertainty of punishments.

Hence it follows, that, without written laws, no society will ever acquire a fixed form of government, in which the power is vested in the whole, and not in any part of the society; and in which the laws are not to be altered but by the will of the whole, nor corrupted by the force of private interest. Experience and reason show us that the probability of human traditions diminishes in proportion as they are distant from their sources. How then can laws resist the inevitable force of time, if therebe not a lasting monument of the social compact.

Hence we see the use of printing, which alone makes the public, and not a few individuals, the guardians and defenders of the laws. It is this art which, by diffusing literature, has gradually dissipated the gloomy spirit of cabal and intrigue. To this art it is owing that the atrocious crimes of our ancestors, who were alternately slaves and tyrants, are become less frequent. Those who are acquainted with the history of the two or three last centuries may observe, how from the lap of luxury and effeminacy have sprung the most tender virtues, humanity, benevolence, and toleration of human errors. They may contemplate the effects of what was so improperly called ancient simplicity and good faith; humanity groaning under implacable superstition, the avarice and ambition of a few staining with human blood the thrones and palaces of kings, secret treasons and public massacres, every noble a tyrant over the people, and the ministers of the gospel of Christ bathing their hands in blood in the name of the God of all mercy. We may talk as we please of the corruption and degeneracy of the present age, but happily we see no such horrid examples of cruelty and oppression.

CHAP. VI.

Of the Proportion between Crimes and Punishments.

IT is not only the common interest of mankind that crimes should not be committed, but that crimes of every kind should be less frequent, in proportion to the evil they produce to society. Therefore the means made use of by the legislature to prevent crimes should be more powerful, in proportion as they are destructive of the public safety and happiness, and as the inducements to commit them are stronger. Therefore there ought to be a fixed proportion between crimes and punishments.

It is impossible to prevent entirely all the disorders which the passions of mankind cause in society. These disorders increase in proportion to the number of people and the opposition of private interests. If we consult history, we shall find them increasing, in every state, with the extent of dominion. In political arithmetic, it is necessary to substitute a calculation of probabilities to mathematical exactness. That force which continually impels us to our own private interest, like gravity, acts incessantly, unless it meets with an obstacle to oppose it. The effects of this force are the confused series of human actions. Punishments, which I would call political obstacles, prevent the fatal effects of private interest, without destroying the impelling cause, which is that sensibility inseparable from man. The legislator acts, in this case, like a skilful architect, who endeavours to counteract the force of gravity by combining the circumstances which may contribute to the strength of his edifice.

The necessity of uniting in society being granted, together with the conventions which the opposite interests of individuals must necessarily require, a scale of crimes may be formed, of which the first degree should consist of those which immediately tend to the dissolution of society, and the last of the smallest possible injustice done to a private member of that society. Between these extremes will be comprehended all actions contrary to the public good which are called criminal, and which descend by insensible degrees, decreasing from the highest to the lowest. If mathematical calculation could be applied to the obscure and infinite combinations of human actions, there might be a corresponding scale of punishments, descending from the greatest to the least; but it will be sufficient that the wise legislator mark the principal divisions, without disturbing the order, left to crimes of the *first* degree be assigned punishments of the *last*. If there were an exact and universal scale of crimes and punishments, we should there have a common measure of the degree of liberty and slavery, humanity and cruelty of different nations.

Any action which is not comprehended in the above mentioned scale will not be called a crime, or punished as such, except by those who have an interest in the denomination. The uncertainty of the extreme points of this scale hath produced a system of morality which contradicts the laws, a multitude of laws that contradict each other, and many which expose the best men to the severest punishments, rendering the ideas of *vice* and *virtue* vague and fluctuating, and even their existence doubtful. Hence that fatal lethargy of political bodies, which terminates in their destruction.

Whoever reads, with a philosophic eye, the history of nations, and their laws, will generally find, that the ideas of virtue and vice, of a good or bad citizen, change with the revolution of ages, not in proportion to the alteration of circumstances, and consequently conformable to the common good, but in proportion to the passions and errors by which the different lawgivers were successively influenced. He will frequently observe that the passions and vices of one age are the foundation of the morality of the following; that violent passion, the offspring of fanaticism and enthusaism, being weakened by time, which reduces all the phenomena of the natural and moral world to an equality, become, by degrees, the prudence of the age, and an useful instrument in the hands of the powerful or artful politician. Hence the uncertainty of our notions of honour and virtue; an uncertainty which will ever remain, because they change with the revolutions of time, and names survive the things they originally signified; they change with the boundaries of states, which are often the same both in physical and moral geography.

Pleasure and pain are the only springs of actions in beings endowed with sensibility. Even amongst the motives which incite men to acts of religion, the invisible legislator has ordained rewards and punishments. From a partial distribution of these will arise that contradiction, so little observed, because so common, I mean that of punishing by the laws the crimes which the laws have occasioned. <u>If an equal punishment be ordained for two crimes that injure society in different degrees, there is nothing to deter men from committing the greater as often as it is attended with greater advantage.</u>

CHAP. VII.

Of estimating the Degree of Crimes.

THE foregoing reflections authorise me to assert that crimes are only to be measured by the injury done to society.

They err, therefore, who imagine that a crime is greater or less according to the intention of the person by whom it is committed; for this will depend on the actual impression of objects on the senses, and on the previous disposition of the mind; both which will vary in different persons, and even in the same person at different times, according to the succession of ideas, passions, and circumstances. Upon that system it would be necessary to form, not only a particular code for every individual, but a new penal law for every crime. Men, often with the best intention, do the greatest injury to society, and, with the worst, do it the most essential services.

Others have estimated crimes rather by the dignity of the person offended than by their consequences to society. If this were the true standard, the smallest irreverence to the Divine Being ought to be punished with infinitely more severity than the assassination of a monarch.

In short, others have imagined, that the greatness of the sin should aggravate the crime. But the fallacy of this opinion will appear on the slightest consideration of the relations between man and man, and between God and man. The relations between man and man are relations of equality. Necessity alone hath produced, from the opposition of private passions and interests, the idea of public utility, which is the foundation of human justice. The other are relations of dependence, between an imperfect creature and his Creator, the most perfect of beings, who has reserved to himself the sole right of being both lawgiver and judge; for he alone can, without injustice, be, at the same time, both one and the other. If he hath decreed eternal punishments for those who disobey his will, shall an insect dare to put himself in the place of divine justice, or pretend to punish for the Almighty, who is himself all sufficient, who cannot receive impressions of pleasure or pain, and who alone, of all other beings, acts without being acted upon? The degree of sin depends on the malignity of the heart, which is impenetrable to finite beings. How then can the degree of sin serve as a standard to determine the degree of crimes? If that were admitted, men may punish when God pardons, and pardon when God condemns; and thus act in opposition to the Supreme Being.

CHAP. VIII.

Of the Division of Crimes.

WE have proved, then, that crimes are to be estimated by *the injury done to society*. This is one of those palpable truths which though evident to the meanest capacity, yet by a combination of circumstances, are only known to a few thinking men in every nation, and in every age. But opinions, worthy only of the despotism of Asia, and passions, armed with power and authority, have, generally by insensible, and sometimes by violent impressions on the timid credulity of men, effaced those simple ideas which perhaps constituted the first philosophy of an infant society. Happily the philosophy of the present enlightened age seems again to conduct us to the same principles, and with that degree of certainty which is obtained by a rational examination and repeated experience.

A scrupulous adherence to order would require, that we should now examine and distinguish the different species of crimes and the modes of punishment; but they are so variable in their nature, from the different circumstances of ages and countries, that the detail would be tiresome and endless. It will be sufficient for my purpose to point out the most general principles, and the most common and dangerous errors, in order to undeceive as well those who, from a mistaken zeal for liberty, would introduce anarchy and confusion, as those who pretend to reduce society in general to the regularity of a covenant.

Some crimes are immediately destructive of society, or its representative; others attack the private security of the life, property, or honour of individuals; and a third class consists of such actions as are contrary to the laws which relate to the general good of the community.

The first, which are of the highest degree, as they are most destructive to society, are called crimes of *leze-majesty*.* Tyranny and ignorance, which have confounded the clearest terms and ideas, have given this appellation to crimes of a different nature, and consequently have establish-

* High Treason.

ed the same punishment for each; and, on this occasion, as on a thousand others, men have been sacrificed victims to a word. Every crime, even of the most private nature, injures society; but every crime does not threaten its immediate destruction. Moral as well as physical actions have their sphere of activity differently circumscribed, like all the movements of nature, by time and space; it is therefore a sophistical interpretation, the common philosophy of slaves, that would confound the limits of things established by eternal truth.

To these succeed crimes which are destructive of the security of individuals. This security being the principal end of all society, and to which every citizen hath an undoubted right, it becomes indispensably necessary, that to these crimes the greatest of punishments should be assigned.

The opinion, that every member of society has a right to do any thing that is not contrary to the laws, without fearing any other inconveniences than those which are the natural consequences of the action itself, is a political dogma, which should be defended by the laws, inculcated by the magistrates, and believed by the people; a sacred dogma, without which there can be no lawful society, a just recompense for our sacrifice of that universal liberty of action common to all sensible beings, and only limited by our natural powers. By this principle our minds become free, active, and vigorous; by this alone we are inspired with that virtue which knows no fear, so different from that pliant prudence, worthy of those only who can bear a precarious existence.

Attempts, therefore, against the life and liberty of a citizen are crimes of the highest nature. Under this head we comprehend not only assassinations and robberies committed by the populace, but by grandees and magistrates, whose example acts with more force, and at a greater distance destroying the ideas of justice and duty among the subjects, and subsituting that of the right of the strongest, equally dangerous to those who exercise it and to those who suffer.

CHAP. IX.

Of Honour.

THERE is a remarkable difference between the civil laws, those jealous guardians of life and property, and the laws of what is called *honour,* which particularly respects the opinion of others. Honour is a term which has been the foundation of many long and brilliant reasonings, without annexing to it any precise or fixed idea. How miserable is the condition of the human mind, to which the most distant and least essential matters, the revolutions of the heavenly bodies, are more distinctly known than the most interesting truths of morality, which are always confused and fluctuating, as they happen to be driven by the gales of passion, or received and transmitted by ignorance! But this will cease to appear strange, if it be considered, that as objects, when too near the eye appear confused, so the too great vicinity of the ideas of morality is the reason why the simple ideas of which they are composed are easily confounded, but which must be separated before we can investigate the phenomina of human sensibility; and the intelligent observer of human nature will cease to be surprised, that so many ties, and such an apparatus of morality, are necessary to the security and happiness of mankind.

Honour, then, is one of those complex ideas which are an aggregate not only of simple ones, but of others so complicated, that, in their various modes of affecting the human mind, they sometimes admit and sometimes exclude part of the elements of which they are composed, retaining only some few of the most common, as many algebraic quantities admit one common divisor. To find this common divisor of the different ideas attached to the word honour, it will be necessary to go back to the original formation of society.

The first laws and the first magistrates owed their existence to the necessity of preventing the disorders which the natural despotism of individuals would unavoidably produce. This was the object of the establishment of society, and was, either in reality or in appearance, the principal design of all codes of laws, even the most pernicious. But the more intimate connexions of men, and the progress of their knowledge, gave rise to an infinite number of necessities and mutual acts of friendship between the members of society. These necessities were not foreseen by the laws, and could not be satisfied by the actual power of each individual. At this epocha began to be established the despotism of opinion, as being the only means of obtaining those benefits which the law could not procure, and of removing those evils against which the laws were no security. It is opinion, that tormentor of the wise and the ignorant, that has exalted the appearance of virtue above virtue itself. Hence the esteem of men becomes not only useful but necessary to every one, to prevent his sinking below the common level. The ambitious man grasps at it, as being necessary to his designs; the vain man sues for it, as a testimony of his merit; the honest man demands it, as his due; and most men consider it as necessary to their existence.

Honour, being produced after the formation of society, could not be a part of the common deposite, and therefore, whilst we act under its influence, we return, for that instant, to a state of nature, and withdraw ourselves from the laws, which, in this case, are insufficient for our protection.

Hence it follows, that, in extreme political liberty, and in absolute despotism, all ideas of honour disappear, or are confounded with others. In the first case, reputation becomes useless from the despotism of the laws; and in the second, the despotism of one man, annulling all civil existence, reduces the rest to a precarious and temporary personality. Honour, then, is one of the fundamental principles of those monarchies which are a limited despotism; and in these, like revolutions in despotic states, it is a momentary return to state of nature and original equality.

CHAP. X.

Of Duelling.

FROM the necessity of the esteem of others have arisen single combats, and they have been established by the anarchy of the laws. They are thought to have been unknown to the ancients, perhaps because they did not assemble in their temples, in their theatres, or with their friends, suspiciously armed with swords; and, perhaps, because single combats were a common spectacle, exhibited to the people by gladiators, who were slaves, and whom freemen disdained to imitate.

In vain have the laws endeavoured to abolish this custom by punishing the offenders with death. A man of honour, deprived of the esteem of others, foresees that he must be reduced either to a solitary existence, insupportable to a social creature, or become the object of perpetual insult; considerations sufficient to overcome the fear of death.

What is the reason that duels are not so frequent among the common people as amongst the great? not only because they do not wear swords, but because to men of that class reputation is of less importance than it is to those of a higher rank, who commonly regard each other with distrust and jealousy.

It may not be without its use to repeat here what has been mentioned by other writers, viz. that the best method of preventing this crime is to punish the aggressor, that is, the person who gave occasion to the duel, and to acquit him who, without any fault on his side, is obliged to defend that which is not sufficiently secured to him by the laws.

CHAP. XI.

Of crimes which disturb the Public Tranquillity.

ANOTHER class of crimes are those which disturb the public tranquillity and the quiet of the citizens; such as tumults and riots in the public streets, which are intended for commerce and the passage of the inhabitants; the discourses of fanatics, which rouse the passions of the curious multitude, and gain strength from the number of their hearers, who, though deaf to calm and solid reasoning, are always affected by obscure and mysterious enthusiasm.

The illumination of the streets during the night at the public expense, guards stationed in different quarters of the city, the plain and moral discourses of religion reserved for the silence and tranquillity of churches, and protected by authority, and harangues in support of the interest of the public, delivered only at the general meetings of the nation, in parliament, or where the sovereign resides, are all means to prevent the dangerous effects of the misguided passions of the people. These should be the principal objects of the vigilance of a magistrate, and which the French call *police;* but if this magistrate should act in an arbitrary manner, and not in conformity to the code of laws, which ought to be in the hands of every member of the community, he opens a door to tyranny, which always surrounds the confines of political liberty.

I do not know of any exception to this general axiom, that *Every member of society should know when he is criminal and when innocent.* If censors, and, in general, arbitrary magistrates, be necessary in any government, it proceeds from some fault in the constitution. The uncertainty of crimes hath sacrificed more victims to secret tyranny than have ever suffered by public and solemn cruelty.

What are, in general, the proper punishments for crimes? Is the punishment of death really *useful*, or necessary for the safety or good order of society? Are tortures and torments consistent with *justice*, or do they answer the *end* proposed by the laws? Which is the best method of preventing crimes? Are the same punishments equally useful at all times? What influence have they on manners? These problems should be solved with that geometrical precision, which the mist of sophistry, the seduction of eloquence, and the timidity of doubt, are unable to resist.

If I have no other merit than that of having first presented to my country, with a greater degree of evidence, what other nations have written and are beginning to practice, I shall account myself fortunate; but if, by supporting the rights of mankind and of invincible truth, I shall contribute to save from the agonies of death one unfortunate victim of tyranny, or of ignorance, equally fatal, his blessing and tears of transport will be a sufficient consolation to me for the contempt of all mankind.

CHAP. XII.

Of the Intent of Punishments.

FROM the foregoing considerations it is evident that the intent of punishments is not to torment a sensible being, nor to undo a crime already committed. Is it possible that torments and useless cruelty, the instrument of furious fanaticism or the impotency of tyrants, can be authorised by a political body, which, so far from being influenced by passion, should be the cool moderator of the passions of individuals? Can the groans of a tortured wretch recal the time past, or reverse the crime he has committed?

The end of punishment, therefore, is no other than to prevent the criminal from doing further injury to society, and to prevent others from committing the like offence. Such punishments, therefore, and such a mode of inflicting them, ought to be chosen, as will make the strongest and most lasting impressions on the minds of others, with the least torment to the body of the criminal.

CHAP. XIII.

Of the Credibility of Witnesses.

TO determine exactly the credibility of a witness, and the force of evidence, is an important point in every good legislation. Every man of common sense, that is, every one whose ideas have some connection with each other, and whose sensations are conformable to those of other men, may be a witness; but the credibility of his evidence will be in proportion as he is interested in declaring or concealing the truth. Hence it appears how frivolous is the reasoning of those who reject the testimony of women, on account of their weakness; how peurile it is not to admit the evidence of those who are under sentence of death, because they are dead in law; and how irrational to exclude persons branded with infamy; for in all these cases they ought to be credited, when they have no interest in giving false testimony.

The credibility of a witness, then, should only diminish in proportion to the hatred, friendship, or connections, subsisting between him and the delinquent. One witness is not sufficient for, whilst the accused denies what the other affirms, truth remains suspended, and the right that every one has to be believed innocent turns the balance in his favour.

The credibility of a witness is the less as the atrociousness of the crime is greater, from the improbability of its having been committed; as in cases of witchcraft, and acts of wanton cruelty. The writers on penal laws have adopted a contrary principle, viz. that the credibility of a witness is greater as the crime is more atrocious. Behold their inhuman maxim, dictated by the most cruel imbecility. *In atrocissimis, leviores conjecturæ sufficiunt, & licit judici jura transgredi.* Let us translate this sentence, that mankind may see one of the many unreasonable principles to which they are ignorantly subject. *In the most atrocious crimes, the slightest conjectures are sufficient, and the judge is allowed to exceed the limits of the law.* The absurd practices of legislators are often the effect of timidity, which is a principal source of the contradictions of mankind. The legislators, (or rather lawyers, whose opinions when alive were interested and venal, but which after their death become of decisive authority, and are the sovereign arbiters of the lives and fortunes of men), terrified by the condemnation of some innocent person, have burdened the law with pompous and useless formalities, the scrupulous observance of which will place anarchical impunity on the throne of justice; at other times, perplexed by atrocious crimes of difficult proof, they imagined themselves under a necessity of superseding the very formalities established by themselves; and thus, at one time with despotic impatience, and at another with feminine timidity, they transform their solemn judgments into a game of hazard.

But, to return: in the case of witchcraft, it is much more probable that a number of men should be deceived than that any person should exercise a power which God hath refused to every created being. In like manner, in cases of wanton cruelty, the presumption is always against the accuser; for no man is cruel without some interest, without some motive of fear or hate. There are no spontaneous or superfluous sentiments in the heart of man; they are all the result of impressions on the senses.

The credibility of a witness may also be diminished by his being a member of a private society, whose customs and principles of conduct are either not known or are different from those of the public. Such a man has not only his own passions, but those of the society of which he is a member.

Finally, the credibility of a witness is null when the question relates to the words of a criminal; for the tone of voice, the gesture, all that precedes, accompanies, and follows the different ideas which men annex to the same words, may so alter and modify a man's discourse, that it is almost impossible to repeat them precisely in the manner in which they were spoken. Besides, violent and uncommon actions, such as real crimes, leave a trace in the multitude of circumstances that attend them, and in their effects; but words remain only in the memory of the hearers, who are commonly negligent or prejudiced. It is infinitely easier, then, to found an accusation on the words than on the actions of a man; for in these the number of circumstances urged against the accused afford him variety of means of justification.

CHAP. XIV.

Of Evidence and the Proofs of a Crime, and of the Form of Judgment.

THE following general theorem is of great use in determining the certainty of a fact. When the proofs of a crime are dependent on each other, that is, when the evidence of each witness, taken separately, proves nothing, or when all the proofs are dependent upon one, the number of proofs neither increase nor diminish the probability of the fact; for the force of the whole is no greater than the force of that on which they depend, and if this fails, they all fall to the ground. When the proofs are independent on each other, the probability of the fact increases in proportion to the number of proofs; for the falshood of the one does not diminish the veracity of another.

It may seem extraordinary that I speak of probability with regard to crimes, which to deserve a punishment, must be certain. But this paradox will vanish when it is considered, that, strictly speaking, moral certainty is only probability, but which is called a certainty, because every man in his senses assents to it from an habit produced by the necessity of acting, and which is anterior to all

speculation. That certainty which is necessary to
decide that the accused is guilty is the very same
which determines every man in the most important
transactions of his life.

The proofs of a crime may be divided into two
classes, perfect and imperfect. I call those perfect
which exclude the possibility of innocence;
imperfect, those which do not exclude this possibility.
Of the first, one only is sufficient for condemnation;
of the second, as many are required
as form a perfect proof; that is to say, that though
each of these, separately taken, does not exclude
the possibility of innocence, it is nevertheless excluded
by their union. It should be also observed,
that the imperfect proofs, of which the accused,
if innocent, might clear himself, and does
not become perfect.

But it is much easier to feel this moral certainty
of proofs than to define it exactly. For this reason,
I think it an excellent law which establishes
assistants to the principal judge, and those chosen
by lot; for that ignorance which judges by its
feelings is less subject to error than the knowledge
or the laws which judges by opinion. Where the
laws are clear and precise, the office of the judge
is merely to ascertain the fact. If, in examining

the proofs of a crime, acuteness and dexterity be required; if clearness and precision be necessary in summoning up the result, to judge of the result itself nothing is wanting but plain and ordinary good sense, a less fallacious guide than the knowledge, of a judge, accustomed to find guilty, and to reduce all things to an artificial system borrowed from his studies. Happy the nation where the knowledge of the law is not a science!

It is an admirable law which ordains that every man shall be tried by his peers; for, when life, liberty and fortune, are in question, the sentiments which a difference of rank and fortune inspires should be silent; that superiority with which the fortunate look upon the unfortunate, and that envy with which the inferior regard their superiors, should have no influence. But when the crime is an offence against a fellow-subject, one half of the judges should be peers to the accused, and the other peers to the person offended: so that all private interest, which, in spite of ourselves, modifies the appearance of objects, even in the eyes of the most equitable, is counteracted, and nothing remains to turn aside the direction of truth and the laws. It is also just that the accused should have the liberty of excluding a certain number of his judges; where this liberty is enjoyed for a long time, without any instance to the contrary, the criminal seems to condemn himself.

All trials should be public, that opinion, which is the best, or perhaps the only cement of society, may curb the authority of the powerful, and the passions of the judge, and that the people may say, 'We are protected by the laws; we are not slaves:' a sentiment which inspires courage, and which is the best tribute to a sovereign who knows his real interest. I shall not enter into particulars. There may be some persons who expect that I should say all that can be said upon this subject; to such what I have already written must be unintelligible.

CHAP. XV.

Of secret Accusations.

SECRET accusations are a manifest abuse, but consecrated by custom in many nations, where, from the weakness of the government, they are necessary. This custom makes men false and treacherous. Whoever suspects another to be an informer, beholds in him an enemy; and from thence mankind are accustomed to disguise their real sentiments; and, from the habit of concealing them from others, they at last even hide them from themselves. Unhappy are those who have arrived at this point! without any certain and fixed principles to guide them, they fluctuate in the vast sea of opinion, and are busied only in escaping the monsters which surround them: to those the present is always embittered by the uncertainty of the future; deprived of the pleasures of tranquillity and security, some fleeting moments of happiness, scattered thinly through their wretched lives, console them for the misery of existing. Shall we, amongst such men, find intrepid soldiers, to defend their king and country? Amongst such men shall we find incorruptible magistrates, who, with the spirit of freedom and patriotic eloquence, will support and explain the true interest of their sovereign; who, with the tributes, offer up at the throne the love and blessing of the people, and thus bestow on the palaces of the great and the humble cottage peace and security, and to the industrious a prospect of bettering their lot, that useful ferment and vital principle of states?

Who can defend himself from calumny, armed with that impenetrable shield of tyranny, secrecy? What a miserable government must that be where the sovereign suspects an enemy in every subject, and, to secure the tranquillity of the public, is obliged to sacrifice the repose of every individual.

By what argument is it pretended that *secret accusations* may be justified? The public safety, say they, and the security and maintenance of the established form of government. But what a strange constitution is that where the government, which hath in its favour not only power, but opinion, still more efficacious, yet fears its own subjects? *The indemnity of the informer;* do not the laws defend him sufficiently? and are there subjects more powerful than the laws? *The necessity of protecting the informer from infamy;* then secret calumny is authorised, and punished only when public. *The nature of the crime;* if actions, indifferent in themselves, or even useful to the public, were called crimes, both the accusation and the trial could never be too secret. But can there be any crime committed against the public which ought not to be publicly punished? I respect all governments; and I speak not of any one in particular. Such may sometimes be the nature of circumstances, that, when abuses are inherent in the constitution, it may be imagined, that to rectify them would be to destroy the constitution itself. But, were I to dictate new laws in a remote corner of the universe, the good of posterity, ever present to my mind, would hold back my trembling hand, and prevent me from authorising *secret accusations*.

Public accusations, says Montésquieu, are more conformable to the nature of a republic, where zeal for the public good is the principal passion of a citizen, than of a monarchy, in which, as this sentiment is very feeble, from the nature of the government, the best establishment is that of *commissioners*, who, in the name of the public, accuse the infractors of the laws. But in all governments, as well in a republic as in a monarchy, the punishment due to the crime of which one accuses another ought to be inflicted on the informer.

CHAP. XVI.

Of Torture.

THE torture of a criminal during the course of his trial is a cruelty consecrated by custom in most nations. It is used with an intent either to make him confess his crime, or to explain some contradictions into which he had been led during his examination, or discover his accomplices, or for some kind of metaphysical and incomprehensible purgation of infamy, or, finally, in order to discover other crimes of which he is not accused, but of which he may be guilty.

No man can be judged a criminal until he be found guilty; nor can society take from him the public protection until it have been proved that he has violated the conditions on which it was granted. What right, then, but that of power, can authorise the punishment of a citizen so long as there remains any doubt of his guilt? This dilemma is frequent. Either he is guilty, or not guilty. If guilty, he should only suffer the punishment ordained by the laws, and torture becomes useless, as his confession is unnecessary. If he be not guilty, you torture the innocent; for, in the eye of the law, every man is innocent whose crime has not been proved. Besides, it is confounding all relations to expect that a man should be both the accuser and accused; and that pain should be the test of truth, as if truth resided in the muscles and fibres of a wretch in torture. By this method the robust will escape, and the feeble be condemned. These are the inconveniencies of this pretended test of truth, worthy only of a cannibal, and which the Romans, in many respects barbarous, and whose savage virtue has been too much admired, reserved for the slaves alone.

What is the political intention of punishments? To terrify and be an example to others. Is this intention answered by thus privately torturing the guilty and the innocent? It is doubtless of importance that no crime should remain unpunished; but it is useless to make a public example of the author of a crime hid in darkness. A crime already committed, and for which there can be no remedy, can only be punished by a political society with an intention that no hopes of impunity should induce others to commit the same. If it be true, that the number of those who from fear or virtue respect the laws is greater than of those by whom they are violated, the risk of torturing an innocent person is greater, as there is a greater probability that, *cæteris paribus*, an individual hath observed, than that he hath infringed the laws.

There is another ridiculous motive for torture, namely, *to purge a man from infamy.* Ought such an abuse to be tolerated in the eighteenth century? Can pain, which is a sensation, have any connection with a moral sentiment, a matter of opinion? Perhaps the rack may be considered as the refiner's furnace.

It is not difficult to trace this senseless law to its origin; for an absurdity, adopted by a whole nation, must have some affinity with other ideas established and respected by the same nation. This custom seems to be the offspring of religion, by which mankind, in all nations and in all ages, are so generally influenced. We are taught by our infallible church, that those stains of sin contracted through human frailty, and which have not deserved the eternal anger of the Almighty, are to be purged away in another life by an incomprehensible fire. Now infamy is a stain, and if the punishments and fire of purgatory can take away all spiritual stains, why should not the pain of torture take away those of a civil nature? I imagine, that the confession of a criminal, which in some tribunals is required as being essential to his condemnation, has a similar origin, and has been taken from the mysterious tribunal of penitence, were the confession of sins is a necessary part of the sacrament. Thus have men abused the unerring light of revelation; and, in the times of tractable ignorance, having no other, they naturally had recourse to it on every occasion, making the most remote and absurd applications. Moreover, infamy is a sentiment regulated neither by the laws nor by reason, but entirely by opinion; but torture renders the victim infamous, and therefore cannot take infamy away.

Another intention of torture is to oblige the supposed criminal to reconcile the contradictions into which he may have fallen during his examination; as if the dread of punishment, the uncertainty of his fate, the solemnity of the court, the majesty of the judge, and the ignorance of the accused, were not abundantly sufficient to account for contradictions, which are so common to men even in a state of tranquillity, and which must necessarily be multiplied by the perturbation of the mind of a man entirely engaged in the thoughts of saving himself from imminent danger.

This infamous test of truth is a remaining

monument of that ancient and savage legislation, in which trials by fire, by boiling water, or the uncertainty of combats, were called *judgments of God;* as if the links of that eternal chain, whose beginning is in the breast of the first cause of all things, could ever be disunited by the institutions of men. The only difference between torture and trials by fire and boiling water is, that the event of the first depends on the will of the accused, and of the second on a fact entirely physical and external: but this difference is apparent only, not real. A man on the rack, in the convulsions of torture, has it as little in his power to declare the truth, as, in former times, to prevent without fraud the effects of fire or boiling water.

Every act of the will is invariably in proportion to the force of the impression on our senses. The impression of pain, then, may increase to such a degree, that, occupying the mind entirely, it will compel the sufferer to use the shortest method of freeing himself from torment. His answer, therefore, will be an effect as necessary as that of fire or boiling water, and he will accuse himself of crimes of which he is innocent: so that the very means employed to distinguish the innocent from the guilty will most effectually destroy all difference between them.

It would be superfluous to confirm these reflections by examples of innocent persons who, from the agony of torture, have confessed themselves guilty: innumerable instances may be found in all nations, and in every age. How amazing that mankind have always neglected to draw the natural conclusion! Lives there a man who, if he has carried his thoughts ever so little beyond the necessities of life, when he reflects on such cruelty, is not tempted to fly from society, and return to his natural state of independence?

The result of torture, then, is a matter of calculation, and depends on the constitution, which differs in every individual, and it is in proportion to his strength and sensibility; so that to discover truth by this method, is a problem which may be better solved by a mathematician than by a judge, and may be thus stated: *The force of the muscles and the sensibility of the nerves of an innocent person being given, it is required to find the degree of pain necessary to make him confess himself guilty of a given crime.*

The examination of the accused is intended to find out the truth; but if this be discovered with so much difficulty in the air, gesture, and countenance of a man at ease, how can it appear in a countenance distorted by the convulsions of torture? Every violent action destroys those small alterations in the features which sometimes disclose the sentiments of the heart.

These truths were known to the Roman legislators, amongst whom, as I have already observed, slaves only, who were not considered as citizens, were tortured. They are known to the English a nation in which the progress of science, superiority in commerce, riches, and power, its natural consequences, together with the numerous examples of virtue and courage, leave no doubt of the excellence of its laws. They have been acknowledged in Sweden, where torture has been abolished. They are known to one of the wisest monarchs in Europe, who, having seated philosophy on the throne by his beneficent legislation, has made his subjects free, though dependent on the laws; the only freedom that reasonable men can desire in the present state of things. In short, torture has not been thought necessary in the laws of armies, composed chiefly of the dregs of mankind, where its use should seem most necessary. Strange phenomenon! that a set of men, hardened by slaughter, and familiar with blood, should teach humanity to the sons of peace.

It appears also that these truths were known,

though imperfectly, even to those by whom torture has been most frequently practised; for a confession made during torture, is null, if it be not afterwards confirmed by an oath, which if the criminal refuses, he is tortured again. Some civilians and some nations permit this infamous *petitio principii* to be only three times repeated, and others leave it to the discretion of the judge; therefore, of two men equally innocent, or equally guilty, the most robust and resolute will be acquitted, and the weakest and most pusillanimous will be condemned, in consequence of the following excellent mode of reasoning. *I, the judge, must find some one guilty. Thou, who art a strong fellow, hast been able to resist the force of torment; therefore I acquit thee. Thou, being weaker, hast yielded to it; I therefore condemn thee. I am sensible, that the confession which was extorted from thee has no weight; but if thou dost not confirm by oath what thou hast already confessed, I will have thee tormented again.*

A very strange but necessary consequence of the use of torture is, that the case of the innocent is worse than that of the guilty. With regard to the first, either he confesses the crime which he has not committed, and is condemned, or he is acquitted, and has suffered a punishment he did not deserve. On the contrary, the person who is really guilty has the most favourable side of the question; for, if he supports the torture with firmness and resolution, he is acquitted, and has gained, having exchanged a greater punishment for a less.

The law by which torture is authorised, says, *Men, be insensible to pain. Nature has indeed given you an irresistible self-love, and an unalienable right of self-preservation ; but I create in you a contrary sentiment, an heroical hatred of yourselves. I command you to accuse yourselves, and to declare the truth, amidst the tearing of your flesh and the dislocation of your bones.*

Torture is used to discover whether the criminal be guilty of other crimes besides those of which he is accused, which is equivalent to the following reasoning. *Thou art guilty of one crime, therefore it is possible that thou mayest have committed a thousand others ; but the affair being doubtful, I must try it by my criterion of truth. The laws order thee to be tormented because thou art guilty, because thou mayest be guilty, and because I choose thou shouldst be guilty.*

Torture is used to make the criminal discover his accomplices; but if it has been demonstrated that it is not at a proper means of discovering truth, how can it serve to discover the accomplices, which is one of the truths required? Will not the man who accuses himself yet more readily accuse others? Besides, is it just to torment one man for the crime of another? May not the accomplices be found out by the examination of the witnesses, or of the criminal; from the evidence, or from the nature of the crime itself; in short, by all the means that have been used to prove the guilt of the prisoner? The accomplices commonly fly when their comrade is taken. The uncertainty of their fate condemns them to perpetual exile, and frees society from the danger of further injury; whilst the punishment of the criminal, by deterring others, answers the purpose for which it was ordained.

CHAP. XVII.

Of pecuniary Punishments.

THERE was a time when all punishments were pecuniary. The crimes of the subjects were the inheritance of the prince. An injury done to society was a favour to the crown; and the sovereign and magistrates, those guardians of the public security, were interested in the violation of the laws. Crimes were tried, at that time, in a court of exchequer, and the cause became a civil suit between the person accused and the crown. The magistrate then had other powers than were necessary for the public welfare, and the criminal suffered other punishments than the necessity of example required. The judge was rather a collector for the crown, an agent for the treasury, than a protector and minister of the laws. But according to this system, for a man to confess himself guilty was to acknowledge himself a debtor to the crown; which was, and is at present (the effects continuing after the causes have ceased) the intent of all criminal causes. Thus, the criminal who refuses to confess his crime, though convicted by the most undoubted proofs, will suffer a less punishment than if he had confessed; and he will not be put to the torture to oblige him to confess other crimes which he might have committed, as he has not confessed the principal. But the confession being once obtained, the judge becomes master of his body, and torments him with a studied formality, in order to squeeze out of him all the profit possible. Confession, then, is allowed to be a convincing proof, especially when obtained by the force of torture; at the same time that an extrajudicial confession, when a man is at ease and under no apprehension, is not sufficient for his condemnation.

All inquiries which may serve to clear up the fact, but which may weaken the pretensions of the crown, are excluded. It was not from compassion to the criminal, or from considerations of humanity, that torments were sometimes spared, but out of fear of losing those rights which at present appear chimerical and inconceivable. The judge becomes an enemy to the accused, to a wretch a prey to the horrors of a dungeon, to torture, to death, and an uncertain futurity, more terrible than all; he inquires not into the truth of the fact, but the nature of the crime; he lays snares to make him convict himself; he fears lest he should not succeed in finding him guilty, and lest that infallibility which every man arrogates to himself should be called in question. It is in the power of the magistrate to determine what evidence is sufficient to send a man to prison; that he may be proved innocent, he must first be supposed guilty. This is what is called an *offensive* prosecution; and such are all criminal proceedings in the eighteenth century, in all parts of our polished Europe. The true prosecution, *for information*, that is, an impartial inquiry into the fact, that which reason prescribes, which military laws adopt, and which Asiatic despotism allows in suits of one subject against another, is very little practised in any courts of justice. What a labyrinth of absurdities! Absurdities which will appear increditable to happier posterity. The philosopher only will be able to read, in the nature of man, the possibility of there ever having been such a system.

CHAP. XX.

Of Acts of violence.

SOME crimes relate to *person*, others to *property*. The first ought to be punished corporally. The great and rich should by no means have it in their power to set a price on the security of the weak and indigent; for then riches, which, under the protection of the laws, are the reward of industry, would become the aliment of tyranny. Liberty is at an end whenever the laws permit that, in certain cases, a man may cease to be *a person*, and become *a thing*. Then will the powerful employ their address to select from the various combinations of civil society all that is in their own favour. This is that magic art which transforms subjects into beasts of burden, and which, in the hands of the strong, is the chain that binds the weak and incautious. Thus it is that in some governments, where there is all the appearance of Liberty, tyranny lies concealed, and insinuates itself into some neglected corner of the constitution, where it gathers strength insensibly. Mankind generally oppose, with resolution, the assaults of barefaced and open tyranny, but disregard the

tion? The laws which require an oath in such a case leave him only the choice of becoming a bad Christian or a martyr. For this reason, oaths become, by degrees, a mere formality, and all sentiments of religion, perhaps the only motive of honesty in the greatest part of mankind, are destroyed. Experience proves their inutility: I appeal to every judge, whether he has ever known that an oath alone has brought truth from the lips of a criminal; and reason tells us, it must be so; for all laws are useless, and in consequence destructive, which contradict the natural feelings of mankind. Such laws are like a dike, opposed directly to the course of a torrent; it is either immediately overwhelmed, or, by a whirlpool formed by itself, it is gradually undermined and destroyed.

CHAP. XIX.

Of the Advantage of immediate Punishment.

THE more immediately after the commission of a crime a punishment is inflicted, the more just and useful it will be. It will be more just, because it spares the criminal the cruel and superfluous torment of uncertainty, which increases in proportion to the strength of his imagination and the sense of his weakness; and because the privation of liberty, being a punishment, ought to be inflicted before condemnation but for as short a time as possible. Imprisonment, I say, being only the means of securing the person of the accused until he be tried, condemned, or acquitted, ought not only to be of as short duration, but attended with as little severity as possible. The time should be determined by the necessary preparation for the trial, and the right of priority in the oldest prisoners. The confinement ought not to be closer than is requisite to prevent his flight, or his concealing the proofs of the crime; and the trial should be conducted with all possible expedition. Can there be a more cruel contrast than that between the indolence of a judge and the painful anxiety of the accused; the comforts and pleasures of an insensible magistrate, and the filth and misery of the prisoner? In general, as I have before observed, *The degree of the punishment, and the consequences of a crime, ought to be so contrived as to have the greatest possible effect on others, with the least possible pain to the delinquent.* If there be any society in which this is not a fundamental principle, it is an unlawful society; for mankind, by their union, originally intended to subject themselves to the least evils possible.

An immediate punishment is more useful; because the smaller the interval of time between the punishment and the crime, the stronger and more lasting will be the association of the two ideas of *crime* and *punishment*; so that they may be considered, one as the cause, and the other as the unavoidable and necessary effect. It is demonstrated, that the association of ideas is the cement which unites the fabric of the human intellect, without which pleasure and pain would be simple and ineffectual sensations. The vulgar, that is, all men who have no general ideas or universal principles, act in consequence of the most immediate and familar associations; but the more remote and complex only present themselves to the minds of those who are passionately attached to a single object, or to those of greater understanding, who have acquired an habit of rapidly comparing together a number of objects, and of forming a conclusion; and the result, that is, the action in consequence, by these means becomes less dangerous and uncertain.

It is, then, of the greatest importance that the punishment should succeed the crime as immediately as possible, if we intend that, in the rude minds of the multitude, the seducing picture of the advantage arising from the crime should instantly awake the attendant idea of punishment. Delaying the punishment serves only to separate these two ideas, and thus affects the minds of the spectators rather as being a terrible sight than the necessary consequence of a crime, the horror of which should contribute to heighten the idea of the punishment.

There is another excellent method of strengthening this important connection between the ideas of crime and punishment; that is, to make the punishment as analogous as possible to the nature of the crime, in order that the punishment may lead the mind to consider the crime in a different point of view from that in which it was placed by the flattering idea of promised advantages.

Crimes of less importance are commonly punished either in the obscurity of a prison, or the criminal is *transported*, to give by his slavery an example to societies which he never offended; an example absolutely useless, because distant from the place where the crime was committed. Men do not, in general, commit great crimes deliberately, but rather in a sudden gust of passion; and they commonly look on the punishment due to a great crime as remote and improbable. The public punishment, therefore, of small crimes will make a greater impression, and, by deterring men from the smaller, will effectually prevent the greater.

little insect that gnaws through the dike, and opens a sure though secret passage to inundation.

CHAP. XXI.

Of the Punishment of the Nobles.

WHAT punishments shall be ordained for the nobles, whose privileges make so great a part of the laws of nations? I do not mean to inquire whether the hereditary distinction between nobles and commoners be useful in any government, or necessary in a monarchy; or whether it be true that they form an intermediate power, of use in moderating the excess of both extremes; or whether they be not rather slaves to to their own body, and to others, confining within a very small circle the natural effects and hopes of industry, like those little fruitful spots scattered here and there in the sandy deserts of Arabia; or whether it be true that a subordination of rank and condition is inevitable or useful in society; and, if so, whether this subordination should not rather subsist between individuals than particular bodies, whether it should not rather circulate through the whole body politic than be confined to one part, and, rather than be perpetual, should it not be incessantly produced and destroyed. Be these as they may, I assert that the punishment of a nobleman should in no wise differ from that of the lowest member of society.

Every lawful distinction, either in honours or riches, supposes previous equality, founded on the laws, on which all the members of society are considered as being equally dependent. We should suppose that men, in renouncing their natural despotism, said, *The wisest and most industrious among us should obtain the greatest honours, and his dignity shall descend to his posterity. The fortunate and happy may hope for greater honours, but let him not therefore be less afraid than others of violating those conditions on which he is exalted.* It is true indeed that no such degrees were ever made in a general diet of mankind, but they exist in the invariable relations of things; nor do they destroy the advantages which are supposed to be produced by the class of nobles, but prevent the inconveniences; and they make the laws respectable, by destroying all hopes of impunity.

It may be objected, that the same punishment inflicted on a nobleman and a plebeian becomes really different from the difference of their education, and from the infamy it reflects on an illustrious family: but I answer, that punishments are to be estimated, not by the sensibility of the criminal, but by the injury done to society, which injury is augmented by the high rank of the offender. The precise equality of a punishment can never be more than external, as it is in proportion to the degree of sensibility which differs in every individual. The infamy of an innocent family may be easily obliterated by some public demonstration of favour from the sovereign, and forms have always more influence than reason on the gazing multitude.

CHAP. XXII.

Of Robbery.

THE punishment of robbery, not accompanied with violence, should be pecuniary. He who endeavours to enrich himself with the property of another should be deprived of part of his own. But this crime, alas! is commonly the effect of misery and despair; the crime of that unhappy part of mankind to whom the right of exclusive property, a terrible and perhaps unnecessary right, has left but a bare existence. Besides, as pecuniary punishments may increase the number of robbers, by increasing the number of poor, and may deprive an innocent family of subsistence, the most proper punishment will be that kind of slavery which alone can be called just; that is, which makes the society, for a time, absolute master of the person and labour of the criminal, in order to oblige him to repair, by this dependence, the unjust despotism he usurped over the property of another, and his violation of the social compact.

When robbery is attended with violence, corporal punishment should be added to slavery. Many writers have shewn the evident disorder which must arise from not distinguishing the punishment due to robbery with violence, and that due to theft or robbery committed with dexterity, absurdly making a sum of money equivalent to a man's life. But it can never be superfluous to repeat, again and again, those truths of which mankind have not profited; for political machines preserve their motion much longer than others, and receive a new impulse with more difficulty. These crimes are in their nature absolutely different, and this axiom is as certain in politics as in mathematics, that between qualities of different natures there can be no similitude.

CHAP. XXIII.

Of Infamy considered as a Punishment.

THOSE injuries which affect the honour, that is, that just portion of esteem which every citizen has a right to expect from others, should be punished with infamy. Infamy is a mark of the public disapprobation, which deprives the object of all consideration in the eyes of his fellow-citizens, of the confidence of his country, and of that fraternity which exists between members of the same society. This is not always in the power of the laws. It is necessary that the infamy inflicted by the laws should be the same with that which results from the relations of things, from universal morality, or from that particular system, adopted by the nation and the laws, which governs the opinion of the vulgar. If, on the contrary, one be different from the other, either the laws will no longer be respected, or the received notions of morality and probity will vanish, in spite of the declamations of moralists, which are always too weak to resist the force of example. If we declare those actions infamous which are in themselves indifferent, we lessen the infamy of those which are really infamous.

The punishment of infamy should not be too frequent, for the power of opinion grows weaker by repetition; nor should it be inflicted on a number of persons at the same time, for the infamy of many resolves itself into the infamy of none.

Painful and corporal punishments should never be applied to fanaticism; for, being founded on pride, it glories in persecution. Infamy and ridicule only should be employed against fanatics: if the first, their pride will be overbalanced by the pride of the people; and we may judge of the power of the second, if we consider that even truth is obliged to summon all her force when attacked by error armed with ridicule. Thus, by opposing one passion to another, and opinion to opinion, a wise legislator puts an end to the admiration of the populace, occasioned by a false principle, the original absurdity of which is veiled by some well deduced consequences.

This is the method to avoid confounding the immutable relations of things, or opposing nature, whose actions, not being limited by time, but operating incessantly, overturn and destroy all those vain regulations which contradict her laws. It is not only in the fine arts that the imitation of nature is the fundamental principle; it is the same in sound policy, which is no other than the art of uniting and directing to the same end the natural and immutable sentiments of mankind.

CHAP. XXIV.

Of Idleness.

A WISE government will not suffer in the midst of labour and industry, that kind of political idleness which is confounded by rigid declaimers with the leisure attending riches acquired by industry, which is of use to an increasing society when confined within proper limits. I call those politically idle, who neither contribute to the good of society by their labour nor their riches; who continually accumulate, but never spend; who are reverenced by the vulgar with stupid admiration, and regarded by the wise with disdain; who, being victims to a monastic life, and deprived of all incitement to that activity which is necessary to preserve or increase its comforts, devote all their vigour to passions of the strongest kind, the passions of opinion. I call not him idle who enjoys the fruits of the virtues or vices of his ancestors, and, in exchange for his pleasures, supports the industrious poor. It is not then the narrow virtue of austere moralists, but the laws, that should determine what species of idleness deserves punishment.

CHAP. XXV.

Of Banishment and Confiscation.

HE who disturbs the public tranquillity, who does not obey the laws, who violates the conditions on which men mutually support and defend each other, ought to be excluded from society, that is, banished.

It seems as if banishment should be the punishment of those who, being accused of an atrocious crime, are probably, but not certainly, guilty. For this purpose would be required a law the least arbitrary and the most precise possible; which should condemn to banishment those who have reduced the community to the fatal alternative either of fearing or punishing them unjustly, still, however, leaving them the sacred right of proving their innocence. The reasons ought to be stronger for banishing a citizen than a stranger, and for the first accusation than for one who hath been often accused.

CRIMES AND PUNISHMENTS.

Should the person who is excluded for ever from society be deprived of his property? This question may be considered in different lights. The confiscation of effects, added to banishment is a greater punishment than banishment alone; there ought then to be some cases, in which, according to the crime, either the whole fortune should be confiscated, or part only, or none at all. The whole should be forfeited, when the law which ordains banishment declares, at the same time, that all connections or relations between the society and the criminal are annihilated. In this case the citizen dies; the man only remains, and, with respect to a political body, the death of the *citizen* should have the same consequences with the death of the *man*. It seems to follow then, that in this case, the effects of the criminal should devolve to his lawful heirs. But it is not on account of this refinement that I disapprove of confiscations. If some have insisted, that they were a restraint to vengeance and the violence of particulars, they have not reflected, that, though punishments be productive of good, they are not, on that account, more just; to be just, they must be necessary. Even an useful injustice can never be allowed by a legislator, who means to guard against watchful tyranny, which, under the flattering pretext of momentary advantages, would establish permanent principles of destruction, and, to procure the ease of a few in a high station, would draw tears from thousands of the poor.

The law which ordains confiscations sets a price on the head of the subject, with the guilty punishes the innocent, and, by reducing them to indigence and despair, tempts them to become criminal. Can there be a more melancholy spectacle than a whole family overwhelmed with infamy and misery from the crime of their chief? a crime, which, if it had been possible, they were restrained from preventing, by that submission which the laws themselves have ordained.

CHAP. XXVI.

Of the Spirit of Family in States.

IT is remarkable, that many fatal acts of injustice have been authorised and approved, even by the wisest and most experienced men, in the freest republics. This has been owing to their having considered the state rather as a society of *families* than of *men*. Let us suppose a nation composed of an hundred thousand men, divided into twenty thousand families of five persons each, including the head or master of the family, its representative. If it be an association of *families*, there will be twenty thousand *men*, and eighty thousand slaves; or if of *men*, there will be an hundred thousand citizens, and not one slave. In the first case we behold a republic, and twenty thousand little monarchies, of which the heads are the sovereigns: in the second the spirit of liberty will not only breath in every public place of the city, and in the assemblies of the nation, but in private houses, where men find the greatest part of their happiness or misery. As laws and customs are always the effect of the habitual sentiments of the members of a republic, if the society be an association of the heads of families, the spirit of monarchy will gradually make its way into the republic itself, as its effects will only be restrained by the opposite interests of each, and not by an universal spirit of liberty and equality. The private spirit of family is a spirit of minuteness, and confined to little concerns. Public spirit, on the contrary, is influenced by general principles, and from facts deduces general rules of utility to the greatest number.

In a republic of families, the children remain under the authority of the father as long as he lives, and are obliged to wait until his death for an existence dependent on the laws alone. Accustomed to kneel and tremble in their tender years, when their natural sentiments were less restrained by that caution, obtained by experience, which is called moderation, how should they resist those obstacles which vice always opposes to virtue in the languor and decline of age, when the despair of reaping the fruits is alone sufficient to damp the vigour of their resolutions?

In a republic, where every man is a citizen, family-subordination is not the effect of compulsion, but of contract; and the sons, disengaged from the natural dependence which the weakness of infancy and the necessity of education required, become free members of society, but remain subject to the head of the family for their own advantage, as in the great society.

In a republic of families, the young people, that is, the most numerous and most useful part of the nation, are at the discretion of their fathers: in a republic of men, they are attached to their parents by no other obligation than that sacred and inviolable one of mutual assistance, and of gratitude for the benefits they have received; a sentiment destroyed not so much by the wickedness of the human heart, as by a mistaken subjection prescribed by the laws.

These contradictions between the laws of families and the fundamental laws of a state are the source of many others between public and private morality, which produce a perpetual conflict in the mind. Domestic morality inspires submission and fear; the other courage and liberty. That instructs a man to confine his beneficence to a small number of persons, not of his own choice; this to extend it to all mankind. That commands a continual sacrifice of himself to a vain idol called the *good of the family*, which is often no real good to any one of those who compose it; this teaches him to consider his own advantage, without offending the laws, or excites him to sacrifice himself for the good of his country, by rewarding him beforehand with the fanaticism it inspires. Such contradictions are the reason that men neglect the pursuit of virtue, which they can hardly distinguish amidst the obscurity and confusion of natural and moral objects. How frequently are men, upon a retrospection of their actions, astonished to find themselves dishonest?

In proportion to the increase of society each member becomes a smaller part of the whole;

and the republican spirit diminishes in the same proportion, if neglected by the laws. Political societies, like the human body, have their limits circumscribed, which they cannot exceed, without disturbing their economy. It seems as if the greatness of a state ought to be inversely as the sensibility and activity of the individuals; if, on the contrary, population and activity increase in the same proportion, the laws will with difficulty prevent the crimes arising from the good they have produced. An overgrown republic can only be saved from despotism by subdividing it into a number of confederate republics. But how is this practicable? By a despotic dictator, who, with the courage of *Sylla*, has as much genius for building up as that Roman had for pulling down. If he be an ambitious man, his reward will be immortal glory? if a philosopher, the blessings of his fellow-citizens will sufficiently console him for the loss of authority, though he should not be insensible to their ingratitude.

In proportion as the sentiments which unite us to the state grow weaker, those which attach us to the objects which more immediately surround us grow stronger; therefore, in the most despotic government, friendships are more durable, and domestic virtues (which are always of the lowest class) are the most common, or the only virtues existing. Hence it appears how confined have been the views of the greatest number of legislators.

CHAP. XXVII.

Of the Mildness of Punishments.

THE course of my ideas has carried me away from my subject, to the elucidation of which I now return. Crimes are more effectually prevented by the *certainty* than the *severity* of punishment. Hence in a magistrate the necessity of vigilance, and in a judge of implacability, which, that it may become an useful virtue, should be joined to a mild legislation. The certainty of a small punishment will make a stronger impression than the fear of one more severe, if attended with the hopes of escaping; for it is the nature of mankind to be terrified at the approach of the smallest inevitable evil, whilst hope, the best gift of Heaven, hath the power of dispelling the apprehension of a greater, especially if supported by examples of impunity, which weakness or avarice too frequently afford.

If punishments be very severe, men are naturally led to the perpetration of other crimes, to avoid the punishment due to the first. The countries and times most notorious for severity of punishments were always those in which the most bloody and inhuman actions and the most atrocious crimes were committed; for the hand of the legislator and the assassin were directed by the same spirit of ferocity, which on the throne dictated laws of iron to slaves and savages, and in private instigated the subject to sacrifice one tyrant to make room for another.

In proportion as punishments become more cruel, the minds of men, as a fluid rises to the same height with that which surrounds it, grow hardened and insensible; and the force of the passions still continuing, in the space of an hundred years the *wheel* terrifies no more than formerly the *prison*. That a punishment may produce the effect required, it is sufficient that the *evil* it occasions should exceed the *good* expected from the crime, including in the calculation the certainty of the punishment, and the privation of the expected advantage. All severity beyond this is superfluous, and therefore tyrannical.

Men regulate their conduct by the repeated impression of evils they know, and not by those with which they are unacquainted. Let us, for example, suppose two nations, in one of which the greatest punishment is *perpetual slavery*, and in the other *the wheel:* I say, that both will inspire the same degree of terror, and that their can be no reasons for increasing the punishments of the first, which are not equally valid for augmenting those of the second to more lasting and more ingenious modes of tormenting, and so on to the most exquisite refinements of a science too well known to tyrants.

There are yet two other consequences of cruel punishments, which counteract the purpose of their institution, which was, to prevent crimes. The *first* arises from the impossibility of establishing an exact proportion between the crime and punishment; for though ingenious cruelty hath greatly multiplyed the variety of torments, yet the human frame can suffer only to a certain degree, beyond which it is impossible to proceed, be the enormity of the crime ever so great. The *second* consequence is impunity. Human nature is limited no less in evil than in good. Excessive barbarity can never be more than temporary, it being impossible that it should be supported by a permanent system of legislation; for if the laws be too cruel, they must be altered, or anarchy and impunity will succeed.

Is it possible without shuddering with horror, to read in history of the barbarous and useless torments that were cooly invented and executed by men who were called sages? Who does not tremble at the thoughts of thousands of wretches, whom their misery, either caused or tolerated by the laws, which favoured the few and outraged the many, had forced in despair to return to a state of nature, or accused of impossible crimes, the fabric of ignorance and superstition, or guilty only of having been faithful to their own principles; who, I say, can, without horror, think of their being torn to pieces, with slow and studied barbarity, by men endowed with the same passions and the same feelings? A delightful spectacle to a fanatic multitude!

CHAP. XXVIII.

Of the Punishment of Death.

THE useless profusion of punishments, which has never made men better, induces me to inquire, whether the punishment of *death* be really just or useful in a well governed state? What *right*, I ask, have men to cut the throats of their fellow-creatures? Certainly not that on which the sovereignty and laws are founded. The laws, as I have said before, are only the sum of the smallest portions of the private liberty of each individual, and represent the general will, which is the aggregate of that of each individual. Did any one ever give to others the right of taking away his life? Is it possible that, in the smallest portions of the liberty of each, sacrificed to the good of the public, can be contained the greatest of all good, life? If it were so, how shall it be reconciled to the maxim which tells us, that a man has no right to kill himself, which he certainly must have, if he could give it away to another?

But the punishment of death is not authorised by any right; for I have demonstrated that no such right exists. It is therefore a war of a whole nation against a citizen, whose destruction they consider as necessary or useful to the general good. But if I can further demonstrate that it is neither necessary nor useful, I shall have gained the cause of humanity.

The death of a citizen cannot be necessary but in one case : when, though deprived of his liberty, he has such power and connections as may endanger the security of the nation; when his existence may produce a dangerous revolution in the established form of government. But, even in this case, it can only be necessary when a nation is on the verge of recovering or losing its liberty, or in times of absolute anarchy, when the disorders themselves hold the place of laws : but in a reign of tranquillity, in a form of government approved by the united wishes of the nation, in a state well fortified from enemies without and supported by strength within, and opinion, perhaps more efficacious, where all power is lodged in the hands of a true sovereign, where riches can purchase pleasures and not authority, there can be no necessity for taking away the life of a subject.

If the experience of all ages be not sufficient to prove, that the punishment of death has never prevented determined men from injuring society, if the example of the Romans, if twenty years' reign of Elizabeth, empress of Russia, in which she gave the fathers of their country an example more illustrious than many conquests bought with blood; if, I say, all this be not sufficient to persuade mankind, who always suspect the voice of reason, and who choose rather to be led by authority, let us consult human nature in proof of my assertion.

It is not the intenseness of the pain that has the greatest effect on the mind, but its continuance; for our sensibility is more easily and more powerfully affected by weak but repeated impressions, than by a violent but momentary impulse. The power of habit is universal over every sensible being. As it is by that we learn to speak, to walk, and to satisfy our necessities, so the ideas of morality are stamped on our minds by repeated impressions. The death of a criminal is a terrible but momentary spectacle, and therefore a less efficacious method of deterring others than the continued example of a man deprived of his liberty, condemned, as a beast of burden, to repair, by his labour, the injury he has done to society, *If I commit such a crime,* says the spectator to himself, *I shall be reduced to that misera-*

ble condition for the rest of my life. A much more powerful preventive than the fear of death which men always behold in distant obscurity.

The terrors of death make so slight an impression, that it has not force enough to withstand the forgetfulness natural to mankind, even in the most essential things, especially when assisted by the passions. Violent impressions surprise us, but their effect is momentary; they are fit to produce those revolutions which instantly transform a common man into a Lacedæmonian or a Persian; but in a free and quiet government they ought to be rather frequent than strong.

The execution of a criminal is to the multitude a spectacle which in some excites compassion mixed with indignation. These sentiments occupy the mind much more than that salutary terror which the laws endeavour to inspire; but, in the contemplation of continued suffering, terror is the only, or at least predominant sensation. The severity of a punishment should be just sufficient to excite compassion in the spectators, as it is intended more for them than for the criminal.

A punishment, to be just, should have only that degree of severity which is sufficient to deter others. Now there is no man who, upon the least reflection, would put in competition the total and perpetual loss of his liberty, with the greatest advantages he could possibly obtain in consequence of a crime. Perpetual slavery, then, has in it all that is necessary to deter the most hardened and determined, as much as the punishment of death. I say it has more. There are many who can look upon death with intrepidity and firmness, some through fanaticism, and others through vanity, which attends us even to the grave; others from a desperate resolution, either to get rid of their misery, or cease to live: but fanaticism and vanity forsake the criminal in slavery, in chains and fetters, in an iron cage, and despair seems rather the beginning than the end of their misery. The mind, by collecting itself and uniting all its force, can, for a moment, repel assailing grief; but its most vigorous efforts are insufficient to resist perpetual wretchedness.

In all nations, where death is used as a punishment, every example supposes a new crime committed; whereas, in perpetual slavery, every criminal affords a frequent and lasting example; and if it be necessary that men should often be witnesses of the power of the laws, criminals should often be put to death: but this supposes a frequency of crimes; and from hence this punishment will cease to have its effect, so that it must be useful and useless at the same time.

I shall be told that perpetual slavery is as painful a punishment as death, and therefore as cruel. I answer, that if all the miserable moments in the life of a slave were collected into one point, it would be a more cruel punishment than any other; but these are scattered through his whole life, whilst the pain of death exerts all its force in a moment. There is also another advantage in the punishment of slavery, which is, that it is more terrible to the spectator than to the sufferer himself; for the spectator considers the sum of all his wretched moments whilst the sufferer, by the misery of the present, is prevented from thinking of the future. All evils are increased by the imagination, and the sufferer finds resources and consolations of which the spectators are ignorant, who judge by their own sensibility of what passes in a mind by habit grown callous to misfortune.

Let us, for a moment, attend to the reasoning of a robber or assassin, who is deterred from violating the laws by the gibbet or the wheel. I am sensible, that to develop the sentiments of one's own heart is an art which education only can teach; but although a villain may not be able to give a clear account of his principles, they nevertheless influence his conduct. He reasons thus: 'What 'are these laws that I am bound to respect, which 'make so great a difference between me and the 'rich man? He refuses me the farthing I ask of 'him, and excuses himself by bidding me have re- 'course to labour, with which he is unacquainted.

Who made these laws? The rich and the great, 'who never deigned to visit the miserable hut of 'the poor, who have never seen him dividing a 'piece of mouldy bread, amidst the cries of his 'famished children and the tears of his wife. 'Let us break those ties, fatal to the greatest 'part of mankind, and only useful to a few indo- 'lent tyrants. Let us attack injustice at its source. 'I will return to my natural state of independence, 'I shall live free and happy on the fruits of my 'courage and industry. A day of pain and re- 'pentance may come, but it will be short; and 'for an hour of grief I shall enjoy years of plea- 'sure and liberty. King of a small number as 'determined as myself, I will correct the mis- 'takes of fortune, and I shall see those tyrants 'grow pale and tremble at the sight of him, 'whom, with insulting pride, they would not suf- 'fer to rank with their dogs and horses.'

Religion then presents itself to the mind of this lawless villain, and, promising him almost a certainty of eternal happiness upon the easy terms of repentance, contributes much to lessen the horror of the last scene of the tragedy.

But he who foresees that he must pass a great number of years, even his whole life, in pain and slavery, a slave to those laws by which he was protected, in sight of his fellow-citizens, with whom he lives in freedom and society, makes an useful comparison between those evils, the uncertainty of his success, and the shortness of the time in which he shall enjoy the fruits of his transgression. The example of those wretches, continually before his eyes, makes a much greater impression on him than a punishment, which instead of correcting, makes him more obdurate.

The punishment of death is pernicious to society, from the example of barbarity it affords. If the passions, or the necessity of war, have taught men to shed the blood of their fellow creatures, the laws, which are intended to moderate the ferocity of mankind, should not increase it by examples of barbarity, the more horrible as this punishment is usually attended with formal pageantry. Is it not absurd, that the laws, which detest and punish homicide, should, in order to prevent murder, publicly commit murder themselves? What are the true and most useful laws? Those compacts and conditions which all would propose and observe in those moments when private interest is silent, or combined with that of the public. What are the natural sentiments of every person concerning the punishment of death? We may read them in the contempt and indignation with which every one looks on the executioner, who is nevertheless an innocent executor of the public will, a good citizen, who contributes to the advantage of society, the instrument of the general security within, as good soldiers are without. What then is the origin of this contradiction? Why is this sentiment of mankind indelible to the scandal of reason? It is, that, in a secret corner of the mind, in which the original impressions of nature are still preserved, men discover a sentiment which tells them, that their lives are not lawfully in the power of any one, but of that necessity only which with its iron sceptre rules the universe.

What must men think, when they see wise magistrates and grave ministers of justice, with indifference and tranquillity, dragging a criminal to death, and whilst a wretch trembles with agony, expecting the fatal stroke, the judge, who has condemned him, with the coldest insensibility, and perhaps with no small gratification from the exertion of his authority, quits his tribunal, to enjoy the comforts and pleasures of life? They will say, 'Ah! those cruel formalities of justice are 'a cloak to tyranny, they are a secret language, a 'solemn veil, intended to conceal the sword by 'which we are sacrificed to the insatiable idol of 'despotism. Murder, which they would repre-'sent to us an horrible crime, we see practised 'by them without repugnance or remorse. Let 'us follow their example. A violent death ap-'peared terrible in their descriptions, but we see 'that it is the affair of a moment. It will be still 'less terrible to him who, not expecting it, es-'capes almost all the pain.' Such is the fatal though absurd reasonings of men who are disposed to commit crimes, on whom the abuse of religion has more influence than religion itself.

If it be objected, that almost all nations in all ages have punished certain crimes with death, I answer, that the force of these examples vanishes when opposed to truth, against which prescription is urged in vain. The history of mankind is an immense sea of errors, in which a few obscure truths may here and there be found.

But human sacrifices have also been common in almost all nations. That some societies only, either few in number, or for a very short time, abstained from the punishment of death, is rather favourable to my argument; for such is the fate of great truths, that their duration is only as a flash of lightning in the long and dark night of error. The happy time is not yet arrived, when truth, as falsehood has been hitherto, shall be the portion of the greatest number.

I am sensible that the voice of one philosopher is too weak to be heard amidst the clamours of a multitude, blindly influenced by custom; but there is a small number of sages scattered on the face of the earth, who will echo to me from the bottom of their hearts; and if these truths should happily force their way to the thrones of princes be it known to them, that they come attended with the secret wishes of all mankind; and tell the sovereign who deigns them a gracious reception, that his fame shall outshine the glory of conquerors, and that equitable posterity will exalt his peaceful trophies above those of a Titus, an Antoninus, or a Trajan.

How happy were mankind if laws were now to be first formed! now that we see on the thrones of Europe benevolent monarchs, friends to the virtues of peace, to the arts and sciences, fathers of their people, though crowned, yet citizens; the increase of whose authority augments the happiness of their subjects, by destroying that intermediate despotism which intercepts the prayers of the people to the throne. If these humane princes have suffered the old laws to subsist, it is doubtless because the are deterred by the numberless obstacles which oppose the subversion of errors established by the sanction of many ages; and therefore every wise citizen will wish for the increase of their authority.

CHAP. XXIX.

Of Imprisonment.

THAT a magistrate, the executor of the laws, should have a power to imprison a citizen, to deprive the man he hates of his liberty, upon frivolous pretences, and to leave his friend unpunished, notwithstanding the strongest proofs of his guilt, is an error as common as it is contrary to the end of society, which is personal security.

Imprisonment is a punishment which differs from all others in this particular, that it necessarily precedes conviction; but this difference does not destroy a circumstance which is essential and common to it with all other punishments, viz. that it should never be inflicted but when ordained by the law. The law should therefore determine the crime, the presumption, and the evidence sufficient to subject the accused to imprisonment and examination. Public report, his flight, his extrajudicial confession, that of an accomplice, menaces, and his constant enmity with the person injured, the circumstances of the crime, and such other evidence, may be sufficient to justify the imprisonment of a citizen. But the nature of this evidence should be determined by the laws, and not by the magistrates, whose decrees are always contrary to political liberty, when they are not particular applications of a general maxim of the public code. When punishments become less severe, and prisons less horrible, when compassion and humanity shall penetrate the iron gates of dungeons, and direct the obdurate and inexorable ministers of justice, the laws may then be satisfied with weaker evidence for imprisonment.

A person accused, imprisoned, tried, and acquitted, ought not to be branded with any degree of infamy. Among the Romans we see that many accused of very great crimes, and afterwards declared innocent, were respected by the people, and honoured with employments in the state. But why is the fate of an innocent person so different in this age? It is because the present system of penal laws presents to our minds an idea of power rather than of justice: it is because the accused and convicted are thrown indiscriminately into the same prison? because imprisonment is rather a punishment than a means of securing the person of the accused; and because the interior power, which defends the laws, and the exterior, which defends the throne and kingdom, are separate, when they should be united. If the first were (under the common authority of the laws) combined with the right of judging, but not however immediately dependent on the magistrate, the pomp that attends a military corps would take off the infamy, which, like all popular opinions, is more attached to the manner and form than to the thing itself, as may be seen in military imprisonment, which, in the common opinion, is not so disgraceful as the civil. But the barbarity and ferocity of our ancestors, the hunters of the north, still subsist among the people in our customs and our laws, which are always several ages behind the actual refinements of a nation.

CHAP. XXX.

Of Prosecution and Prescription.

THE proofs of the crime being obtained, and the certainty of it determined, it is necessary to allow the criminal time and means for his justification; but a time so short as not to diminish that promptitude of punishment, which, as we have shewn, is one of the most powerful means of preventing crimes. A mistaken humanity may object to the shortness of the time, but the force of the objection will vanish if we consider that the danger of the innocent increases with the defects of the legislation.

The time for inquiry and for justification should be fixed by the laws, and not by the judge, who, in that case, would become legislator. With regard to atrocious crimes, which are long remembered, when they are once proved, if the criminal have fled, no time should be allowed; but in less considerable and more obscure crimes, a time should be fixed, after which the delinquent should be no longer uncertain of his fate: for, in the latter case, the length of time, in which the crime is almost forgotten, prevents the example of impunity, and allows the criminal to amend, and become a better member of society.

General principles will here be sufficient, it being impossible to fix precisely the limits of time for any given legislation, or for any society in any particular circumstance. I shall only add, that, in a nation willing to prove the utility of moderate punishment, laws which, according to the nature of the crime, increase or diminish the time of inquiry and justification, considering the imprisonment or the voluntary exile of the criminal as a part of the punishment, will form an easy division of a small number of mild punishments for a great number of crimes.

But it must be observed, the time for inquiry and justification should not increase in direct proportion to the atrociousness of crimes; for the probability of such crimes having been committed is inversely as their atrociousness. Therefore the time for inquiring ought, in some cases, to be diminished, and that for justification increased, *et vice versa.* This may appear to contradict what I have said above, namely, that equal punishments may be decreed by unequal crimes, by considering the time allowed the criminal or the prison as a punishment.

In order to explain this idea, I shall divide crimes into two classes. The first comprehends homicide, and all greater crimes; the second crimes of an inferior degree. This distinction is founded in human nature. The preservation of life is a natural right; the preservation of property is a right of society. The motives that induce men to shake off the natural sentiment of compassion, which must be destroyed before great crimes can be committed, are much less in number than those by which, from the natural desire of being happy, they are instigated to violate a right which is not founded in the heart of man, but is the work of society. The different degrees of probability in these two classes, require that they should be regulated on different principles. In the greatest crimes, as they are less frequent, and the probability of the innocence of the accused being greater, the time allowed him for his justification should be greater, and the time of inquiry less. For, by hastening the definitive sentence, the flattering hopes of impunity are destroyed, which are more dangerous as the crime is more atrocious. On the contrary, in crimes of less importance, the probability of the innocence being less, the time of inquiry should be greater, and that of justification less, as impunity is not so dangerous.

But this division of crimes into two classes

should not be admitted, if the consequences of impunity were in proportion to the probability of the crime. It should be considered, that a person accused, whose guilt or innocence is not determined for want of proofs, may be again imprisoned for the same crime, and be subject to a new trial, if fresh evidence arises within the time fixed.

This is, in my opinion, the best method of providing at the same time for the security and liberty of the subject, without favouring one at the expense of the other; which may easily happen, since both these blessings, the unalienable and equal patrimony of every citizen, are liable to be invaded, the one by open or disguised despotism, and the other by tumultuous and popular anarchy.

CHAP. XXXI.

Of Crimes of difficult Proof.

WITH the forgoing principles in view, it will appear astonishing, that reason hardly ever presided at the formation of the laws of nations; that the weakest and most equivocal evidence, and even conjectures, have been thought sufficient proof for crimes the most atrocious, (and therefore most improbable,) the most obscure and chimerical; as if it were the interest of the laws and the judge not to enquire into the truth, but to prove the crime; as if there were not a greater risk of condemning an innocent person, when the probability of his guilt is less.

The generality of men want that vigour of mind and resolution which are as necessary for great crimes as for great virtues, and which at the same time produce both the one and the other in those nations which are supported by the activity of their government, and a passion for the public good. For in those which subsist by their greatness or power, or by the goodness of their laws, the passions, being in a weaker degree, seem calculated rather to maintain than to improve the form of government. This naturally leads us to an important conclusion, viz. that great crimes do not always produce the destruction of a nation.

There are some crimes which, though frequent in society, are of difficult proof, a circumstance admitted as equal to the probability of the innocence of the accused. But as the frequency of these crimes is not owing to their impunity so much as to other causes, the danger of their passing unpunished is of less importance, and therefore the time of examination and prescription may be equally diminished. These principles are different from those commonly received; for it is in crimes which are proved with the greatest difficulty, such as adultery and sodomy, that presumptions, half proofs, &c. are admitted; as if a man could be half innocent, and half guilty, that is, half punishable and half absolvable. It is in these cases that torture should exercise its cruel power on the person of the accused, the witnesses, and even his whole family, as, with unfeeling indifference, some civilians have taught, who pretend to dictate laws to nations.

Adultery is a crime which, politically considered, owes its existence to two causes, viz. pernicious laws, and the powerful attraction between the sexes. This attraction is similar in many circumstances to gravity, the spring of motion in the universe. Like this, it is diminished by distance; one regulates the motions of the body, the other of the soul. But they differ in one respect; the force of gravity decreases in proportion to the obstacles that oppose it, the other gathers strength and vigour as the obstacles increase.

If I were speaking to nations guided only by the laws of nature, I would tell them, that there is a considerable difference between adultery and all other crimes. Adultery proceeds from an abuse of that necessity which is constant and universal in human nature; a necessity anterior to the formation of society, and indeed the founder of society itself; whereas all other crimes tend to the destruction of society, and arise from momentary passions, and not from a natural necessity. It is the opinion of those who have studied history and mankind, that this necessity is constantly in the same degree in the same climate. If this be true, useless, or rather pernicious, must all laws and customs be which tend to diminish the sum total of the effects of this passion. Such laws would only burden one part of society with the additional necessities of the other; but, on the contrary, wise are the laws which, following the natural course of the river, divide the stream into a number of equal branches, preventing thus both sterility and inundation.

Conjugal fidelity is always greater in proportion as marriages are more numerous and less difficult. But, when the interest or pride of families, or paternal authority, not the inclination of the parties, unite the sexes, gallantry soon breaks the slender ties, in spite of common moralists, who exclaim against the effect, whilst they pardon the cause. But these reflections are useless to those who, living in the true religion, act from sublimer motives, which correct the eternal laws of nature.

The act of adultery is a crime so instantaneous, so mysterious, and so concealed by the veil which the laws themselves have woven, a veil necessary indeed, but so transparent as to heighten rather than conceal the charms of the object, the opportunities are so frequent, and the danger of discovery so easily avoided, that it were much easier for the laws to prevent this crime, than to punish it when committed.

To every crime which, from its nature, must frequently remain unpunished, the punishment is an incentive. Such is the nature of the human mind, that difficulties, if not unsurmountable, nor too great for our natural indolence, embellish the object, and spur us on to the pursuit. They are so many barriers that confine the imagination to the object, and oblige us to consider it in every point of view. In this agitation, the mind naturally inclines and fixes itself to the most agreeable part, studiously avoiding every idea that might create disgust.

The crime of sodomy, so severely punished by the laws, and for the proof of which are employed tortures, which often triumph over innocence itself, has its source much less in the passions of man in a free and independent state than in society and a slave. It is much less the effect of a satiety in pleasures, than of that education which in order to make men useful to others, begins by making them useless to themselves. In those public seminaries, where ardent youth are carefully excluded from all commerce with the other sex, as the vigour of nature blooms, it is consumed in a manner not only useless to mankind, but which accelerates the approach of old age.

The murder of bastard children is, in like manner, the effect of a cruel dilemma, in which a woman finds herself, who has been seduced through weakness, or overcome by force. The alternative is, either her own infamy, or the death of a being who is incapable of feeling the loss of life. How can she avoid preferring the last to the inevitable misery of herself and her unhappy infant! The best method of preventing this crime would be effectually to protect the weak woman from that tyranny which exaggerates all vices that cannot be concealed under the cloak of virtue.

I do not pretend to lessen that just abhorrence which these crimes deserve, but to discover the sources from whence they spring; and I think I may draw the following conclusion: *That the punishment of a crime cannot be just, (that is necessary,) if the laws have not endeavoured to prevent that crime by the best means which times and circumstances would allow.*

CHAP. XXXII.

Of Suicide.

SUICIDE is a crime which seems not to admit of punishment, properly speaking; for it cannot be inflicted but on the innocent, or upon an insensible dead body. In the first case, it is unjust and tyrannical, for political liberty supposes all punishments entirely personal; in the second, it has the same effect, by way of example, as the scourging a statue. Mankind love life too well; the objects that surround them, the seducing phantom of pleasure, and hope, that sweetest error of mortals, which makes men swallow such large draughts of evil, mingled with a very few drops of good, allure them too strongly, to apprehend that this crime will ever be common from its unavoidable impunity. The laws are obeyed through fear of punishment, but death destroys all sensibility. What motive then can restrain the desperate hand of suicide?

He who kills himself does a less injury to society than he who quits his country for ever; for the other leaves his property behind him, but this carries with him at least a part of his substance. Besides, as the strength of society consists in the number of citizens, he who quits one nation to reside in another, becomes a double loss. This then is the question: whether it be advantageous to society that its members should enjoy the unlimited privilege of migration?

Every law that is not armed with force, or which, from circumstances, must be ineffectual, should not be promulgated. Opinion, which reigns over the minds of men, obeys the slow and indirect impressions of the legislator, but resists them when violently and directly applied; and useless laws communicate their insignificance to the most salutary, which are regarded more as obstacles to be surmounted than as safeguards of the public good. But further, our preceptions being limited, by enforcing the observance of laws which are evidently useless, we destroy the influence of the most salutary.

From this principle a wise dispenser of public happiness may draw some useful consequences, the explanation of which would carry me too far from my subject, which is to prove the inutility of making the nation a prison. Such a law is vain; because, unless inaccessible rocks or impassable seas divide the country from all others, how will it be possible to secure every point of the circumference, or how will you guard the guards themselves? Besides, this crime once committed cannot be punished; and to punish it before hand would be to punish the intention and not the action, the will, which is entirely out of the power of human laws. To punish the absent by confiscating his effects, besides the facility of collusion, which would inevitably be the case, and which, without tyranny, could not be prevented, would put a stop to all commerce with other nations. To punish the criminal when he returns, would be to prevent him from repairing the evil he had already done to society, by making his absence perpetual. Besides, any prohibition would increase the desire of removing, and would infallibly prevent strangers from settling in the country.

What must we think of a government which has no means but fear to keep its subjects in their own country, to which, by the first impressions of their infancy, they are so strongly attached. The most certain method of keeping men at home is to make them happy; and it is the interest of every state to turn the balance, not only of commerce, but of felicity, in favour of its subjects. The pleasures of luxury are not the principle sources of this happiness, though, by preventing the too great accumulation of wealth in a few hands, they become a necessary remedy against the too great inequality of individuals, which always increases with the progress of society.

When the populousness of a country does not increase in proportion to its extent, luxury favours despotism? for where men are most dispersed there is least industry, and where there is least industry the dependence of the poor upon the luxury of the rich is greatest, and the union of the oppressed against the oppressors is least to be feared. In such circumstances, rich and powerful men more easily command distinction, respect, and service, by which they are raised to a greater height above the poor; for men are more independent the less they are observed, and are least observed when most numerous. On the contrary, when the number of people is too great in proportion to the extent of a country, luxury is a check to despotism; because it is a spur to industry, and because the labour of the poor affords so many pleasures to the rich, that they disregard the luxury of ostentation, which would remind the people of their dependence. Hence we see, that, in vast and depopulated states, the luxury of ostentation prevails over that of convenience;

but in countries more populous, the luxury of convenience tends constantly to diminish the luxury of ostentation.

The pleasures of luxury have this inconvenience, that though they employ a great number of hands, yet they are only enjoyed by a few, whilst the rest who do not partake of them, feel the want more sensibly on comparing their state with that of others. Security and liberty, restrained by the laws, are the basis of happiness, and when attended by these, the pleasures of luxury favour population, without which they become the instruments of tyranny. As the most noble and generous animals fly to solitude and inaccessible deserts, and abandon the fertile plains to man their greatest enemy, so men reject pleasure itself when offered by the hand of tyranny.

But, to return:—If it be demonstrated that the laws which imprison men in their own country are vain and unjust, it will be equally true of those which punish suicide; for that can only be punished after death, which is in the power of God alone; but it is no crime with regard to man, because the punishment falls on an innocent family. If it be objected, that the consideration of such a punishment may prevent the crime, I answer, that he who can calmly renounce the pleasure of existence, who is so weary of life as to brave the idea of eternal misery, will never be influenced by the more distant and less powerful considerations of family and children.

CHAP. XXXIII.

Of Smuggling.

SMUGGLING is a real offence against the sovereign and the nation; but the punishment should not brand the offender with infamy, because this crime is not infamous in the public opinion. By inflicting infamous punishments for crimes that are not reputed so, we destroy that idea where it may be useful. If the same punishment be decreed for killing a pheasant as for killing a man, or for forgery, all difference between those crimes will shortly vanish. It is thus that moral sentiments are distroyed in the heart of man; sentiments, the work of many ages and of much bloodshed; sentiments that are so slowly and with so much difficulty produced, and for the establishment of which such sublime motives and such an apparatus of ceremonies were thought necessary.

This crime is owing to the laws themselves; for the higher the duties the greater is the advantage, and consequently the temptation; which temptation is increased by the facility of perpetration, when the circumference that is guarded is of great extent, and the merchandise prohibited is small in bulk. The seizure and loss of the goods attempted to be smuggled, together with those that are found along with them, is just! but it would be better to lessen the duty, because men risk only in proportion to the advantage expected.

This crime being a theft of what belongs to the prince, and consequently to the nation, why is it not attended with infamy? I answer, that crimes which men consider as productive of no bad consequences to themselves, do not interest them sufficiently to excite their indignation. The generality of mankind, upon whom remote consequences make no impression, do not see the evil that may result from the practice of smuggling, especially if they reap from it any present advantage. They only perceive the loss sustained by the prince. They are not then interested in refusing their esteem to the smuggler, as to one who has committed a theft or a forgery, or other crimes, by which they themselves may suffer, from this evident principle, that a sensible being only interests himself in those evils with which he is acquainted.

Shall this crime then, committed by one who has nothing to lose, go unpunished? No. There are certain species of smuggling, which so particularly affect the revenue, a part of government so essential, and managed with so much difficulty, that they deserve imprisonment, or even slavery; but yet of such a nature as to be proportioned to the crime. For example, it would be highly unjust, that a smuggler of tobacco should suffer the same punishment with a robber or assassin; but it would be most conformable to the nature of the offence, that the produce of his labour should be applied to the use of the crown, which he intended to defraud.

CHAP. XXXIV.

Of Bankrupts.

THE necessity of good faith in contracts, and the support of commerce, oblige the legislator to secure for the creditors the persons of bankrupts. It is, however, necessary to distinguish between the fraudulent and the honest bankrupt. The fraudulent bankrupt should be punished in the same manner with him who adulterates the coin; for, to falsify a piece of coin, which is a pledge of the mutual obligations between citizens, is not a greater crime than to violate the obligations themselves. But the bankrupt who, after a strict examination, has proved before proper judges, that either the fraud or losses of others, or misfortunes unavoidable by human prudence, have stripped him of his substance, upon what barbarous pretence is he thrown into prison, and thus deprived of the only remaining good, the melancholy enjoyment of mere liberty? Why is he ranked with criminals, and in despair compelled to repent of his honesty? Conscious of his innocence, he lived easy and happy under the protection of those laws which, it is true, he violated, but not intentionally; laws dictated by the avarice of the rich, and accepted by the poor, seduced by that universal and flattering hope, which makes men believe that all unlucky accidents are the lot of others, and the most fortunate only their share. Mankind, when influenced by the first impressions, love cruel laws, although, being subject to them themselves, it is the interest of every person that they should be as mild as possible; but the fear of being injured is always more prevalent than the intention of injuring others.

But, to return to the honest bankrupt: let his debt, if you will, not be considered as cancelled, till the payment of the whole; let him be refused the liberty of leaving the country without leave of his creditors, or of carrying into another nation that industry which, under a penalty, he should be obliged to employ for their benefit; but what pretence can justify the depriving an innocent though unfortunate man of his liberty, without the least utility to his creditors?

But, say they, the hardships of confinement will induce him to discover his fraudulent transactions; an event that can hardly be supposed, after a rigorous examination of his conduct and affairs. But if they are not discovered, he will escape unpunished. It is, I think, a maxim of government, that the importance of the political inconveniencies arising from the impunity of a crime, are directly as the injury to the public, and inversely as the difficulty of proof.

It will be necessary to distinguish fraud, attended with aggravating circumstances, from simple fraud, and that from perfect innocence. For the first, let there be ordained the same punishment as for forgery; for the second a less punishment, but with the loss of liberty; and if perfectly honest, let the bankrupt himself choose the method of re-establishing himself, and of satisfying his creditors; or, if he should appear not to have been strictly honest, let that be determined by his creditors · but these distinctions should be fixed by the laws, which alone are impartial, and not by the arbitrary and dangerous prudence of judges.*

With what ease might a sagacious legislator

---

* It may be alledged that the interest of commerce and property should be secured; but commerce and property are not the end of the social compact, but the means of obtaining that end; and to expose all the members of society to cruel laws, to preserve them from evils necessarily occasioned by the infinite combinations which result from the actual state of political societies, would be to make the end subservient to the means, a paralogism in all sciences, and particularly in politics. In the former editions of this work I myself fell into this error, when I said that the honest bankrupt should be kept in custody, as a pledge for his debts, or employed as a slave to work for his creditors. I am ashamed of having adopted so cruel an opinion. I have been accused of impiety; I did not deserve it. I have been accused of sedition; I deserved it as little. But I insulted all the rights of humanity, and was never reproached.

prevent the greatest part of fraudulent bankruptcies, and remedy the misfortunes that befal the honest and industrious! A public register of all contracts, with the liberty of consulting it allowed to every citizen: a public fund, formed by a contribution of the opulent merchants, for the timely assistance of unfortunate industry, were establishments that could produce no real inconveniencies, and many advantages. But, unhappily, the most simple, the easiest, yet the wisest laws, that wait only for the nod of the legislator, to diffuse through nations wealth, power, and felicity, laws which would be regarded by future generations with eternal gratitude, are either unknown or rejected. A restless and trifling spirit, the timid prudence of the present moment, a distrust and aversion to the most useful novelties, possess the minds of those who are empowered to regulate the actions of mankind.

CHAP. XXXV.

Of Sanctuaries.

ARE sanctuaries just? Is a convention between nations mutually to give up their criminals useful?

In the whole extent of a political state there should be no place independent of the laws. Their power should follow every subject, as the shadow follows the body. Sanctuaries and impunity differ only in degree, and as the effect of punishments depends more on their certainty than their greatness, men are more strongly invited to crimes by sanctuaries than they are deterred by punishment. To increase the number of sanctuaries is to erect so many little sovereignties; for where the laws have no power, new bodies will be formed in opposition to the public good, and a spirit established contrary to that of the state. History informs us, that from the use of sanctuaries have arisen the greatest revolutions in kingdoms and in opinions.

Some have pretended, that in whatever country a crime, that is, an action contrary to the laws of society, be committed, the criminal may be justly punished for it in any other; as if the character of subject were indelible, or synonymous with or worse than that of slave; as if a man could live in one country and be subject to the laws of another, or be accountable for his actions to two sovereigns, or two codes of laws often contradictory. There are also those who think, that an act of cruelty committed, for example, at Constantinople may be punished at Paris, for this abstracted reason, that he who offends humanity should have enemies in all mankind, and be the object of universal execration; as if judges were to be the knights-errant of human nature in general, rather than guardians of particular conventions between men. The place of punishment can certainly be no other than that where the crime was committed; for the necessity of punishing an individual for the general good, subsists there, and there only. A villain, if he has not broke through the conventions of a society, of which, by my supposition, he was not a member, may be feared, and by force banished and excluded from that society, but ought not to be formally punished by the laws, which were only intended to maintain the social compact, and not to punish the intrinsic malignity of actions.

Whether it be useful that nations should mutually deliver up their criminals? Although the certainty of there being no part of the earth where crimes are not punished, may be a means of preventing them, I shall not pretend to determine this question, until laws more conformable to the necessities, and rights of humanity, and until milder punishments, and the abolition of the arbitrary power of opinion, shall afford security to virtue and innocence when oppressed; and until tyranny shall be confined to the plains of Asia, and Europe acknowledge the universal empire of reason by which the interests of sovereigns and subjects are best united.

CHAP. XXXVI.

Of Rewards for apprehending or killing Criminals.

LET us now inquire, whether it be advantageous to society, to set a price on the head of a criminal, and so to make of every citizen an executioner? If the offender hath taken refuge in another state, the sovereign encourages his subjects to commit a crime, and to expose themselves to a just punishment; he insults that nation, and authorises the subjects to commit on their neighbours similar usurpations. If the criminal still remain in his own country, to set a price upon his head is the strongest proof of the weakness of the government. He who has strength to defend himself will not purchase the assistance of another. Besides, such an edict confounds all the ideas of virtue and morality, already too wavering in the mind of man. At one time treachery is punished by the laws, at another encouraged. With one hand the legislator strengthens the ties of kindred and friendship, and with the other rewards the violation of both. Always in contradiction with himself, now he invites the suspecting minds of men to mutual confidence, and now he plants distrust in every heart. To prevent one crime he gives birth to a thousand. Such are the expedients of weak nations, whose laws are like temporary repairs to a tottering fabric. On the contrary, as a nation becomes more enlightened, honesty and mutual confidence become more necessary, and are daily tending to unite with sound policy. Artifice, cabal, and obscure and indirect actions are more easily discovered, and the interest of the whole is better secured against the passions of the individual.

Even the times of ignorance, when private virtue was encouraged by public morality, may afford instruction and example to more enlightened ages. But laws which reward treason excite clandestine

138   AN ESSAY ON

war and mutual distrust, and oppose that necessary union of morality and policy which is the foundation of happiness and universal peace.

CHAP. XXXVII.

Of Attempts, Acomplices, and Pardon.

THE laws do not punish the intention; nevertheless, an attempt, which manifests the intention of committing a crime, deserves a punishment, though less, perhaps, than if the crime were actually perpetrated. The importance of preventing even attempts to commit a crime sufficiently authorises a punishment; but, as there may be an interval of time between the attempt and the execution, it is proper to reserve the greater punishment for the actual commission, that even after the attempt there may be a motive for desisting.

In like manner, with regard to the accomplices, they ought not to suffer so severe a punishment as the immediate perpetrator of the crime: but this for a different reason. When a number of men unite, and run a common risk, the greater the danger, the more they endeavour to distribute it equally. Now, if the principals be punished more everely than the accessaries, it will prevent the danger from being equally divided, and will increase the difficulty of finding a person to execute the crime, as his danger is greater by the difference of the punishment. There can be but one exception to this rule, and that is, when the principal receives a reward from the accomplices. In that case, as the difference of the danger is compensated, the punishment should be equal. These reflections may appear too refined to those who do not consider, that it is of great importance that the laws should leave the associates as few means as possible of agreeing among themselves.

In some tribunals a pardon is offered to an accomplice in a great crime, if he discover his associates. This expedient has its advantages and disadvantages. The disadvantages are, that the law authorises treachery, which is detested even by the villains themselves, and introduces crimes of cowardice, which are much more pernicious to a nation than crimes of courage. Courage is not common, and only wants a benevolent power to direct it to the public good. Cowardice, on the contrary, is a frequent, self-interested, and contagious evil, which can never be improved into a virtue. Besides, the tribunal which has recourse to this method, betrays its fallibility, and the laws their weakness, by imploring the assistance of those by whom they are violated.

The advantages are, that it prevents great crimes, the effects of which being public, and the perpetrators concealed, terrify the people. It also contributes to prove, that he who violates the laws, which are public conventions, will also violate private compacts. It appears to me that a general law, promising a reward to every accomplice who discovers his associates, would be better than a special declaration in every particular case; because it would prevent the union of those villains, as it would inspire a mutual distrust, and each would be afraid of exposing himself alone to danger. The accomplice, however, should be pardoned, on condition of transportation.—— But it is in vain that I torment myself with endeavouring to extinguish the remorse I feel in attempting to induce the sacred laws, the monument of public confidence, the foundation of human morality, to authorise dissimulation and perfidy. But what an example does it offer to a nation to see the interpreters of the laws break their promise of pardon, and on the strength of learned subtleties, and to the scandal of public faith, drag him to punishment who hath accepted of their invitation! Such examples are not uncommon, and this is the reason that political society is regarded as a complex machine, the springs of which are moved at pleasure by the most dexterous or most powerful.

CHAP. XXXVIII.

Of suggestive Interrogations.

THE laws forbid *suggestive interrogations;* that is, according to the civilians, questions which, with regard to the circumstances of the crime, are *special* when they should be *general;* or, in other words, those questions which, having an immediate reference to the crime, suggests to the criminal an immediate answer. Interrogations, according to the law, ought to lead to the fact indirectly and obliquely, but never directly or immediately. The intent of this injunction is, either that they should not suggest to the accused an immediate answer that might acquit him, or that they think it contrary to nature that a man should accuse himself. But whatever be the motive, the laws have fallen into a palpable contradiction, in condemning suggestive interrogations, whilst they authorise torture. Can there be an interrogation more suggestive than pain? Torture will suggest to a robust villain an obstinate silence, that he may exchange a greater punishment for a less; and to a feeble man confession, to relieve him from the present pain, which affects him more than the apprehension of the future. If a special interrogation be contrary to the right of nature, as it obliges a man to accuse himself, torture will certainly do it more effectually. But men are influenced more by the names than the nature of things.

He who obstinately refuses to answer the interrogatories deserves a punishment, which should be fixed by the laws, and that of the severest kind; the criminals should not, by their silence, avade the example which they owe the public. But this punishment is not necessary when the guilt of the criminal is indisputable; because in that case interrogation is useless, as is likewise his confession, when there are, without it, proofs sufficient. This last case is most common, for experience shews, that in the greatest number of criminal prosecutions the culprit pleads not guilty.

CHAP. XXXIX.

Of a particular Kind of Crimes.

THE reader will perceive that I have omitted speaking of a certain class of crimes which has covered Europe with blood, and raised up those horrid piles, from whence, amidst clouds of whirling smoke, the groans of human victims, the crackling of their bones, and the frying of their still panting bowels, were a pleasing spectacle and agreeable harmony to the fanatic multitude. But men of understanding will perceive, that the age and country in which I live, will not permit me to inquire into the nature of this crime. It were too tedious and foreign to my subject to prove the necessity of a perfect uniformity of opinions in a state, contrary to the examples of many nations; to prove that opinions, which differ from one another only in some subtile and obscure distinctions, beyond the reach of human capacity, may nevertheless disturb the public tranquillity, unless one only religion be established by authority; and that some opinions, by being contrasted and opposed to each other, in their collision strike out the truth; whilst others, feeble in themselves, require the support of power and authority. It would, I say, carry me too far, where I to prove, that, how odious soever is the empire of force over the opinions of mankind, from whom it only obtains dissimulation followed by contempt, and although it may seem contrary to the spirit of humanity and brotherly love, commanded us by reason, and authority, which we more repect, it is nevertheless necessary and indispensable. We are to believe, that all these paradoxes are solved beyond a doubt, and are conformable to the true interest of mankind, if practised by a lawful authority. I write only of *crimes* which violate the laws of nature and the social contract, and not of *sins*, even the temporal punishments of which must be determined from other principles than those of limited human philosophy.

CHAP. XL.

Of false Ideas of Utility.

A PRINCIPAL source of errors and injustice are false ideas of utility. For example: that legislator has false ideas of utility who considers particular more than general conveniencies, who had rather command the sentiments of mankind than excite them, and dares say to reason, ' Be thou a slave;' who would sacrifice a thousand real advantages to the fear of an imaginary or trifling inconvenience; who would deprive men of the use of fire for fear of their being burnt, and of water for fear of their being drowned; and who knows of no means of preventing evil but by destroying it.

The laws of this nature are those which forbid to wear arms, disarming those only who are not disposed to commit the crime which the laws mean to prevent. Can it be supposed, that those who have the courage to violate the most sacred laws of humanity, and the most important of the code, will respect the less considerable and arbitrary injunctions, the violation of which is so easy, and of so little comparative importance? Does not the execution of this law deprive the subject of that personal liberty, so dear to mankind and to the wise legislator? and does it not subject the innocent to all the disagreeable circumstances that should only fall on the guilty? It certainly makes the situation of the assaulted worse, and of the assailants better, and rather encourages than prevents murder, as it requires less courage to attack unarmed than armed persons.

It is a false idea of utility that would give to a multitude of sensible beings that symmetry and order which inanimate matter is alone capable of receiving; to neglect the present, which are the only motives that act with force and constancy on the multitude, for the more distant, whose impressions are weak and transitory, unless increased by that strength of imagination so very uncommon among mankind. Finally, that is a false idea of utility which, sacrificing things to names, separates the public good from that of individuals.

There is this difference between a state of society and a state of nature, that a savage does no more mischief to another than is necessary to procure some benefit to himself: but a man in society is sometimes tempted, from a fault in the laws, to injure another without any prospect of advantage. The tyrant inspires his vassals with fear and servility, which rebound upon him with double force, and are the cause of his torment. Fear, the more private and domestic it is, the less dangerous is it to him who makes it the instrument of his happiness; but the more it is public, and the greater number of people it affects, the greater is the probability that some mad, desperate, or designing person will seduce others to his party by flattering expectations; and this will be the more easily accomplished as the danger of the enterprise will be divided amongst a greater number, because the value the unhappy set upon their existence is less, as their misery is greater.

CHAP. XLI.

Of the Means of preventing Crimes.

IT is better to prevent crimes than to punish them. This is the fundamental principle of good legislation, which is the art of conducting men to the *maximum* of happiness, and to the *minimum* of misery, if we may apply this mathematical expression to the good and evil of life. But the means hitherto employed for that purpose are generally inadequate, or contrary to the end proposed. It is impossible to reduce the tumultuous activity of mankind to absolute regularity; for, amidst the various and opposite attractions of pleasure and pain, human laws are not sufficient entirely to prevent disorders in society. Such, however is the chimera of weak men, when invested with authority. To prohibit a number of indifferent actions is not to prevent the crimes which they may produce, but to create new ones, it is to change at will the ideas of virtue and vice, which, at other times, we are told, are eternal and immutable. To what a situation should we be reduced if every thing were to be forbidden that might possibly lead to a crime? We must be

CRIMES AND PUNISHMENTS.   149

deprived of the use of our senses : for one motive that induces a man to commit a real crime, there are a thousand which excite him to those indifferent actions which are called crimes by bad laws. If then the probability that a crime will be committed be in proportion to the number of motives, to extend the sphere of crimes will be to increase that probability. The generality of laws are only exclusive privileges, the tribute of all to the advantages of a few.

Would you prevent crimes? Let the laws be clear and simple, let the entire force of the nation be united in their defence, let them be intended rather to favour every individual than any particular classes of men, let the laws be feared, and the laws only. The fear of the laws is salutary, but the fear of men is a fruitful and fatal source of crimes. Men enslaved are more voluptuous, more debauched, and more cruel than those who are in a state of freedom. These study the sciences, the interest of nations, have great objects before their eyes, and imitate them ; but those, whose views are confined to the present moment, endeavour, amidst the distraction of riot and debauchery, to forget their situation ; accustomed to the uncertainty of all events, for the laws determine none, the consequences of their crimes become problematical, which gives an additional force to the strength of their passions.

In a nation indolent from the nature of the climate, the uncertainty of the laws confirms and increases men's indolence and stupidity. In a voluptuous but active nation, this uncertainty occasions a multiplicity of cabals and intrigues, which spread distrust and diffidence through the hearts of all, and dissimulation and treachery are the foundation of their prudence. In a brave and powerful nation, this uncertainty of the laws is at last destroyed, after many oscillations from liberty to slavery, and from slavery to liberty again.

CHAP. XLII.

Of the Sciences.

WOULD you prevent crimes? Let liberty be attended with knowledge. As knowledge extends, the disadvantages which attend it diminish and the advantages increase. A daring impostor, who is always a man of some genius, is adored by the ignorant populace, and despised by men of understanding. Knowledge facilitates the comparison of objects, by shewing them in different points of view. When the clouds of ignorance are dispelled by the radiance of knowledge, authority trembles, but the force of the laws remains immoveable. Men of enlightened understanding must necessarily approve those useful conventions which are the foundation of public safety; they compare with the highest satisfaction, the inconsiderable portion of liberty of which they are deprived with the sum total sacrificed by others for their security; observing that they have only given up the pernicious liberty of injuring their fellow-creatures, they bless the throne, and the laws upon which it is established.

It is false that the sciences have always been

prejudicial to mankind. When they were so, the evil was inevitable. The multiplication of the human species on the face of the earth introduced war, the rudiments of arts, and the first laws, which were temporary compacts, arising from necessity, and perishing with it. This was the first philosophy, and its few elements were just, as indolence and want of sagacity in the early inhabitants of the world preserved them from error.

But necessities increasing with the number of mankind, stronger and more lasting impressions were necessary to prevent their frequent relapses into a state of barbarity, which became every day more fatal. The first religious errors, which peopled the earth with false divinities, and created a world of invisible beings to govern the visible creation, were of the utmost service to mankind. The greatest benefactors to humanity were those who dared to deceive, and lead pliant ignorance to the foot of the altar. By presenting to the minds of the vulgar things out of the reach of their senses, which fled as they pursued, and always eluded their grasp which as they never comprehended, they never despised, their different passions were united, and attached to a single object. This was the first transition of all nations from their savage state. Such was the necessary, and perhaps the only bond of all societies at their first formation. I speak not of the chosen people of God, to whom the most extraordinary miracles and the most signal favours supplied the place of human policy. But as it is the nature of error to subdivide itself *ad infinitum*, so the pretended knowledge which sprung from it, transformed mankind into a blind fanatic multitude, jarring and destroying each other in the labyrinth in which they were inclosed: hence it is not wonderful that some sensible and philosophic minds should regret the ancient state of barbarity. This was the first epocha, in which knowledge, or rather opinions, were fatal.

The second may be found in the difficult and terrible passage from error to truth, from darkness to light. The violent shock between a mass of errors useful to the few and powerful, and the truths so important to the many and the weak, with the fermentation of passions excited on that occasion, were productive of infinite evils to unhappy mortals. In the study of history, whose principal periods, after certain intervals, much resemble each other, we frequently find, in the necessary passage from the obsurity of ignorance to the light of philosophy, and from tyranny to liberty, its natural consequence, one generation sacrificed to the happiness of the next. But when this flame is extinguished, and the world delivered from its evils, truth, after a very slow progress, sits down with monarchs on the throne, and is worshipped in the assemblies of nations. Shall we then believe, that light diffused among the people is more destructive than darkness, and that the knowledge of the relation of things can ever be fatal to mankind?

Ignorance may indeed be less fatal than a small degree of knowledge, because this adds to the evils of ignorance, the inevitable errors of a confined view of things on this side the bounds of truth; but a man of enlightened understanding, appointed guardian of the laws, is the greatest blessing that a sovereign can bestow on a nation. Such a man is accustomed to behold truth, and not to fear it; unacquainted with the greatest part of those imaginary and insatiable necessities which so often put virtue to the proof, and accustomed to contemplate mankind from the most elevated point of view, he considers the nation as his family, and his fellow-citizens as brothers; the distance between the great and the vulgar appears to him the less as the number of mankind he has in view is greater.

The philosopher has necessities and interests

unknown to the vulgar, and the chief of these is not to belie in public the principles he taught in obscurity, and the habit of loving virtue for its own sake. A few such philosophers would constitute the happiness of a nation; which however would be but of short duration, unless by good laws the number were so increased as to lessen the probability of an improper choice.

CHAP. XLIII.

Of Magistrates.

ANOTHER method of preventing crimes is, to make the observance of the laws, and not their violation, the interest of the magistrate.

The greater the number of those who constitute the tribunal, the less is the danger of corruption; because the attempt will be more difficult, and the power and temptation of each individual will be proportionably less. If the sovereign, by pomp and the austerity of edicts, and by refusing to hear the complaints of the oppressed, accustom his subjects to respect the magistrates more than the laws, the magistrates will gain indeed, but it will be at the expense of public and private security.

CHAP XLIV.

Of Rewards.

YET another method of preventing crimes is, to reward virtue. Upon this subject the laws of all nations are silent. If the rewards proposed by academies for the discovery of useful truths have increased our knowledge, and multiplied good books, is it not probable, that rewards, distributed by the beneficent hand of a sovereign, would also multiply virtuous actions. The coin of honour is inexhaustible, and is abundantly fruitful in the hands of a prince who distributes it wisely.

CHAP. XLV.

Of Education.

FINALLY, the most certain method of preventing crimes is, to perfect the system of educaion. But this is an object too vast, and exceeds my plan; an object, if I may venture to declare it, which is so intimately connected with the nature of government, that it will always remain a barren spot, cultivated only by a few wise men.

A great man, who is persecuted by that world he hath enlightened, and to whom we are indebted for many important truths, hath most amply detailed the principal maxims of useful education. This chiefly consists in presenting to the mind a small number of select objects, in substituting the originals for the copies both of physical and moral phenomena, in leading the pupil to virtue by the easy road of sentiment, and in withholding him from evil by the infallible power of necessary inconveniences, rather than by command, which only obtains a counterfeit and momentary obedience.

CHAP. XLVI.

Of Pardons.

AS punishments become more mild, clemency and pardon are less necessary. Happy the nation in which they will be considered as dangerous! Clemency, which has often been deemed a sufficient substitute for every other virtue in sovereigns, should be excluded in a perfect legislation, where punishments are mild, and the proceedings in criminal cases regular and expeditious. This truth will seem cruel to those who live in countries where, from the absurdity of the laws and the severity of punishments, pardons and the clemency of the prince are necessary. It is indeed one of the noblest prerogatives of the throne, but, at the same time, a tacit disapprobation of the laws. Clemency is a virtue which belongs to the legislator, and not to the executor of the laws; a virtue which ought to shine in the code, and not in private judgment. To shew mankind that crimes are sometimes pardoned, and that punishment is not the necessary consequence, is to nourish the flattering hope of impunity, and is the cause of their considering every punishment inflicted as an act of injustice and oppression. The prince in pardoning gives up the public security in favour of an individual, and, by his ill-judged benevolence, proclaims a public act of impunity. Let, then, the executors of the laws be inexorable, but let the legislator be tender, indulgent, and humane. He is a wise architect who erects his edifice on the foundation of self-love, and contrives that the interest of the public shall be the interest of each individual, who is not obliged, by particular laws and irregular proceedings, to seperate the public good from that of individuals, and erect the image of public felicity on the basis of fear and distrust; but, like a wise philosopher, he will permit his bretheren to enjoy in quiet that small portion of happiness, which the immense system, established by the first cause, permits them to taste on this earth, which is but a point in the universe.

A small crime is sometimes pardoned if the person offended chooses to forgive the offender. This may be an act of good nature and humanity, but it is contrary to the good of the public: for although a private citizen may dispense with satisfaction for the injury he has received, he cannot remove the necessity of example. The right of punishing belongs not to any individual in particular, but to society in general, or the sovereign. He may renounce his own portion of this right, but cannot give up that of others.

CHAP. XLVII.

Conclusion.

I CONCLUDE with this reflection, that the severity of punishments ought to be in proportion to the state of the nation. Among a people hardly yet emerged from barbarity, they should be most severe, as strong impressions are required; but, in proportion as the minds of men become softened by their intercourse in society, the severity of punishments should be diminished, if it be intended that the necessary relation between the object and the sensation should be maintained.

From what I have written results the following general theorem, of considerable utility, though not conformable to custom, the common legislator of nations:

That a punishment may not be an act of violence, of one, or of many, against a private member of society, it should be public, immediate, and necessary, the least possible in the case given, proportioned to the crime, and determined by the laws.

A COMMENTARY

ON THE ESSAY ON

CRIMES AND PUNISHMENTS.

CHAP. I.

The Circumstances that occasioned this Commentary.

MY mind was full of reflexions arising from the perusal of the little work on crimes and punishments, which is in moral science, what the few remedies capable of alleviating our bodily complaints are in medicine. I flattered myself that this work would soften what remained of barbarism in the criminal jurisprudence of a great many nations; I hoped for some reformation in human nature itself; when I was informed that a girl of eighteen years of age, handsome, possessed of useful talents, and of a very respectable family, had just been hung in one of the provinces.

Her crime was, having yielded to illicit love, and in afterwards abandoning her child, the fruit of the connexion. This unhappy girl, flying from her parents house, was taken in labour, and delivered, alone and without assistance, near a brook. The feeling of shame, which in the sex is a powerful passion, gave her strength to return to the house of her father, and to conceal her situation. She left her child exposed; it was found the next day; the mother ascertained; condemned to death, and executed.

The *first fault* of this girl should have been considered by her family as a family secret, or met with protection from the law; because the seducer should be bound to repair the evil he had done; because weakness has a claim to indulgence; because every feeling is in favor of a woman whose concealed pregnancy often exposes her life, at the same time that discovery of her condition would destroy her reputation; and, because the difficulty of providing for the support of her child is a very great additional misfortune.

Her *second fault* was more criminal; she abandoned the fruit of her weakness, and exposed it to the risk of perishing.

But because a child died, was it obsolutely necessary to destroy the mother? She did not murder it; she flattered herself that some passenger would have compassion for an innocent being; she might even have had an intention of returning with the view of finding her child, and affording it every necessary assistance. This feeling, too, is so natural, that its existence in the heart of a mother ought to be presumed. I know the law is positive against a woman under the circumstances above related, in the province to which I alluded; but at the same time is not this law unjust, inhuman, and pernicious? *Unjust*, because it makes no distinction between the woman who murders, and she who abandons her child; *inhuman*, because it cruelly inflicts the punishment of death on an unfortunate being, whose only crime is weakness and anxiety to conceal her miserable situation; *pernicious*, because it forcibly tears from society a fellow being capable of adding to the subjects of the state, and that too, in a province where they are sensible of the want of inhabitants. Charity has not as yet provided, in that province, houses of reception, where children who are exposed may receive necessary care: where charity is wanting, law is always cruel. It would certainly be better to *prevent* these unhappy occurrences, which happen but too often, than simply to rest satisfied with punishing them. The real object of jurisprudence is to prevent the commission of crimes, not to punish with death the weaker sex, especially when it is evident that their faults are unaccompanied with malice, and who are more than adequately punished by the feelings of their own hearts.

Furnish, as far as possible, to those who may be tempted to do evil, the means of avoiding it, and you will have fewer criminals to punish.

CHAP. II.

Of Punishments.

THE unfortunate occurrence, and the severe law, with which I have been so struck, induced me to cast my eyes on the criminal code of nations. The humane author of the " Essay on Crimes and Punishments " had but too much reason to complain, that the latter was, too frequently, disproportioned to the former, and sometimes even detrimental to the state they were intended to serve.

Ingenious punishments, to imagine which the human mind seems to have exhausted itself in order to render death terrible, seem rather the inventions of tyranny than of justice.

The punishment of the *wheel*, was first introduced into Germany during times of anarchy, when those who usurped regal power wished to terrify, by the studied preparation of unheard-of torment, whosoever should dare to make an attempt upon their authority. In England, they ripped up the belly of a man convicted of *high treason*, tore out his heart, dashed it in his face, and then threw it upon the fire. And what, very frequently, constituted the crime of *high treason*? During the civil wars, a faithful adherence to an unfortunate monarch; and, sometimes, the expression of an opinion upon the doubtful rights of a conqueror. Time, however, rendered their manners milder; they continue notwithstanding, to tear out the heart, but it is always after the death of the criminal. The apparatus death is dreadful; but the death itself is easy, if death can ever be said to be easy.

CHAP. III.

Of the Punishments of Heretics.

THE denunciation of the punishment of death against those who differed from the established church in certain points of doctrine, was peculiarly the act of tyranny. No christian emperor, before the time of the tyrant Maximus, ever thought of condemning any man to punishment, merely on account of controversial points. It is true, that it was two Spanish bishops who pursued to death the Priscillianists under Maximus; but it is also not the less true, that this tyrant was willing to gratify the ruling party by shedding the blood of heretics. Barbarity and justice were viewed by him with equal indifference. Jealous of Theodosius, who was also a Spaniard, he flattered himself with the idea of depriving him of the empire of the east, having already usurped that of the west. Theodosius was detested for his cruelties; but he understood the art of gaining to his party the heads of the church. Maximus was desirous, by displaying the same zeal, of attaching the Spanish bishops to his faction. He flattered both the old and the new religion; he was a man as treacherous as inhuman, as indeed were all those, who, at this period, aspired to or obtained the empire. The govenrment of this vast portion of the world was similar to that of Algiers at the present day. The soldiery created and dethroned the emperors; they selected them often from among the natives of their country regarded as barbarous. Theodosius opposed to his antagonist other barbarians from Seythia: it was he who filled the armies with Goths, and who raised up Alaric the conqueror of Rome. In this horrible state of confusion, the empire belonged to him who could strengthen his party most effectually, by any and every means in his power.

Maximus, just had procured the assassination, at Lyons, of Gratian, the colleague of Theodosius; and meditated the destruction of Valentinian the 2d. who, while yet a child had been nominated as the successor of Gratian-at Rome. He assembled at Treves a powerful army composed of Gauls and Germans. He was also leveying troops in Spain, when two Spanish bishops Idacio and Ithacus or Itacius,· men who possessed much influence, came and demanded of him the blood of Priscillian and of all his adherents, who were persuaded that souls are emanations from God; that the trinity does not include three Hypostases; and who, moreover, carried their sacrilegious doings so far as actually to fast on sundays. Maximus, half pagan, half christian, was soon aware of the enormity of these crimes. The holy bishops, Idacio and Itacius, also obtained permission to torture Priscillian and his adherents before they put them to death. They were both present at the executions in order to see that all things were regularly conducted; and they returned home praising God, and numbering Maximus, the defender of the faith, among the saints. But Maximus being defeated by Theodosius, and afterwards murdered at the feet of his vanquisher, had not the honor to be canonized. It is proper, at the same time, to remark, that St. Martin, bishop of Tours, who was a truly good man, solicited the pardon of Priscillian; but being himself accused of being a heretic, he returned to Tours for fear of being put to the torture at Trevis.

As for Priscillian, he had the consolation, after being hanged however, of being looked upon by his followers as a Martyr. They celebrated the day of his canonization, and they would probably do so to this day, if there were any Priscillianists remaining in the world.

This example made the whole church tremble;

but, soon after, it was not only successfully imitated, but even surpassed. Priscillianists had preshed by the sword, by the halter, and by stoning to death: a young lady of quality, *suspected*, of having fasted on a sunday, was *only* stoned to death at Bordeaux. These punishments, however, appeared too mild; it having been duly proved, that God required heretics to be roasted alive by a slow fire. The convincing argument offered in support of this opinion was, that it was in that manner that God himself punishes them in another world; to which they added that all princes, and all representatives of princes, including therein all petty magistrates, were the images of God in this sublunary world!

In pursuance of this principle they every where burned all witches and sorcerers; such personages being manifestly under the empire of the devil; and extended the same charity to all heterodox christians, who were deemed more criminal and dangerous than even sorcerers themselves.

The precise nature of the heresy, with which the priests whom king Robert (the son of Hugh,) and Constance his wife ordered to be burned in their presence at Orleans, in 1022, were contaminated, is not known. How indeed it should be known, there being at that time none but some few scholars and monks who could read, is not easy to determine. This fact, however, is well established, that Robert and his wife satiated their eyes with the view of this most abominable spectacle—One of these sectaries had been confessor to Constance, who thought, that she could in no way better repair the misfortune of having confessed herself to a heretic, than by seeing him devoured by the flames. Custom ripens into law: from that period down to the present day, the church has continued to burn those who were, or who at least appeared to be, blackened by the crime of erroneous opinion.

CHAP. IV.

Of the extirpation of Heresies.

WE ought, it appears to me, in matters of heresy, to distinguish between *opinion* and *faction*. From the first ages of christianity, opinions have been divided on the subject of religious duty. The christians of Alexandria did not agree, on many points, with those of Antioch. The Achaians were at variance with the Asiatics. This diversity of opinion has existed in every age, and, in all probability, will continue forever. Jesus Christ, who alone could have united all the faithful in one opinion, did not do so; it is fair, therefore, to presume, that such was not his intention; but, that his design was rather to exercise all his churches in performances of charity, and acts of indulgence towards each other, by permitting the establishment of different systems, which, however, should all unite in acknowledging him as their Lord and Master. These sects, for a long period of time, either tolerated by the Roman emperors, or, concealed in quiet obscurity, were unable to persecute each other, as they were all in equal subjection to the Roman magistrates; they only possessed the right of disputation. When persecuted by the magistrates, they all claimed the privilege of nature; "suffer us, said they, to worship our God in peace; do not deny to us, the liberty you grant to the Jews." Every sect at the present day has a right to hold the same language to their oppressors. They can say, with justice, to those who have granted privileges to the Jews; "Treat us, at least, as you treat these children of Jacob; let us, like them, worship God according to the dictates of our own consciences; our opinions will injure your kingdonm no more than Judaism. You tolerate the enemies of Jesus Christ; tolerate, at least, us, who are his worshipers, and who differ from yourselves, only in some trifling theological subtilties—Do not deprive yourselves of useful subjects. It is of importance to you to possess our exertions in your navy, in your manufactories, and in the cultivation of the soil; and, it is of trifling import to you that we differ in some few articles of faith. It is *our* labor that *you* stand in need of, and we do not wish *you* to adopt *our* catechism."

Faction is a very different thing. It always happens, and that necessarily too, that a persecuted sect degenerates into a faction. The oppressed naturally unite and encourage each other. They are more industrious in the work of strengthening their party, than the reigning sect are in the business of extermination. They crush or are crushed. Precisely so it happened (after the persecution set on foot in the year 303 by Galerius) during the two last years of the reign of Dioclesian. The christians having been favoured by Dioclesian for a period of eighteen years, were too numerous, and too rich to be exterminated: they attached themselves to Constantius Chlorus, they fought for his son Constantine, and an entire revolution in the empire was the consequence.

Trifling events may be compared with those

that are great, when they are directed by the same spirit. Similar revolutions took place in Holland, Scotland, and Switzerland. When Ferdinand and Isabella drove out of Spain the Jews, who were settled there before the then reigning house, before the Moors, and even before the Carthaginians, the Jews, if they had been as warlike as they were rich, and could have made arrangements with the Arabs, might easily have brought about a revolution in Spain. In short, no sect ever succeeded in producing a change in the government of a country until despair furnished them with the means. Mahomet himself succeeded, simply because he was driven from Mecca, and a reward offered for his head.

Would you prevent then any sect from overturning a state-exercise toleration: imitate the wise conduct by which England, Germany, and Scotland are regulated. Government has but one choice to make with regard to the mode of treating a new sect; that of putting to death, without mercy, the chiefs of the sect, and all their adherents, men, women, and children; or, that of tolerating them when the sect is numerous. The first method is that of a monster; the other that of a sage. Bind every subject to the state with the chains of his own interest. Let the Quaker and the Turk find their advantage in living under the protection of your laws. Religion is a matter between God and man; the performance of civil duties a question between Government and the people.

CHAP. V

Of Blasphemy and Profanation.

LOUIS the 9th. king of France, who, for his virtue, was numbered among the saints, made a law against blasphemers. He condemned them to a new species of punishment; that of having the tongue pierced with a red hot iron. This was a kind of lex talionis; the member that had sinned suffered the whole punishment. But it was very difficult to determine what was really blasphemy. In the transports of rage, in the excitement of joy, even in common conversation, expressions often escape from a man, which, strictly speaking, are merely expletives; such as the *Selah* and the *Vah* of the Hebrews; the *Pol* and the *Ædepol* of the Latins; and the *per Deos immortales*, an expression made use of every moment without the least intention of swearing by the immortal Gods.

The words called *oaths* and *blasphemy*, usually consist of vague terms, which may be variously interpreted. The law punishing those making use of them, seems to have been taken from the Jewish commandment, which says " *Thou shalt not take the name of God in vain.*" The best interpreters think that this law has relation only to perjury. And there is great reason to believe they are right, as the word *shave* in the original, which is translated *in vain*, strictly speaking signifies *perjury*. Now who can discover perjury, in the words *cadedis sangbleu, ventrebleu, corbleu.*

The Jews swore by the life of God. "*as the Lord liveth.*" It was a common phrase; so that the only thing forbidden, was, *lying*, at the time that God was called upon to witness the truth of what the party said.

Philip Augustus, in 1181, condemned such of the *nobility* of his kingdom as should pronouce the words *têblebleu, ventrebleu, corbleu, sangbleu*, to pay a fine, and ordered *commoners* to be drowned. The first part of this ordinance seems puerile, the second was abominable. It was an outrage on human nature to drown a commoner for the fault which a nobleman expiated by paying a few pence of the money of those times. The natural consequence was, that this extraodinary law remained unexecuted, as indeed did many other laws, particularly during the time that the king was under a sentence of excommunication, and his kingdom laid under an interdict by Pope Celestine the 3d. St. Louis, inflamed with holy zeal, gave orders, that whosoever should pronounce the indecent words we have mentioned, should have, either his tongue bored, or his upper lip cut off. But a respectable citizen of Paris having lost his tongue in consequence of the punishment, complained to Pope Innocent the IV, who represented with decision to the king, that the punishment was too severe for the crime. The king for the future desisted from this severity. Happy had it been for mankind, if the popes had never affected any other superiority over kings.

The ordinance of Louis the 14th. of the year 1666, directs: "that whosoever shall be convicted of having sworn by, and blasphemed the holy name of God, of his most holy Mother, or of his Saints, shall, for the first offence, pay a fine; for the second, third, and fourth offence, a double, triple and quadruple fine; for the fifth offence, be put in the stocks; for the sixth, shall stand in the pillory, and have the upper lip cut off; and for the seventh offence have the tongue entirely cut out."

This law appears to be wise and humane; it inflicts a severe punishment on a sevenfold repetition of the crime, a thing scarcely to be anticipated with regard to those more daring profanations designated by the term of *sacrilege.* Our compilations of criminal jurisprudence, where *decisions* are reported, which, however we are not to consider as *laws*, make mention only of the crime of church-robbery: and there is no positive law on this subject condemning the criminal to the flames. The laws also are silent on the subject of public impiety; either, because such folly was not anticipated, or, that there exists great difficulty in specifying the acts necessary to constitute the offence. This crime is therefore left, as far as regards punishment, to the discretion of the judges. Justice, however, should not leave any offence undefined, or its punishment arbitrary.

In cases that occur so rarely, what, it may be asked, is the proper course for a judge to pursue? He ought to consider the age of the offender, the nature of his offence, the degree of evil disposition and obstinacy manifested, the public scandal to which it may have given rise, and, particularly, whether or no there exists a necessity for a terrible public example. *Pro qualitate personæ proque rei conditione et temporis et ætatis et sexûs, vel severius vel clementius statuendem.** And if the law does not expressly provide the punishment of death for the crime—What Judge can deem himself bound to authorise its infliction? If there *must* be a punishment; if the *law* is silent; a judge should, without hesitation, award the mildest punishment in his power—Because he himself is a man.

Sacrilegious profanations are never committed, except by young and dissipated men: would you punish them for this crime as severely as if they had committed murder on a brother? Their youth itself pleads in their favor. They can not even dispose of *their property;* because they are supposed to want the maturity of judgment necessary to anticipate the probable consequences of an imprudent transaction; it is, therefore, reasonable to suppose, that they cannot properly estimate the results of an impious sally.

Would you treat a dissolute young man, who, in a frolic, had profaned, not stolen, a sacred image, with the severity that you treated a *Brinvilliers*, who poisoned her father and all his family?

There is no existing law that condemns the

---

* Tit. XIII. *Ad legem Julian*

unhappy wretch—You create one in order to subject him to the severest punishment. He deserves an exemplary chastisement; but does he merit tortures, at the thought of which nature shudders, in addition to a violent death?

But he has sinned against God; true, he has, most grievously. Deal with him, then, as God would deal. If penitent;—God forgives him. Cause him, therefore, bitterly to repent; but, at the same time, forgive him also.

Your own illustrious Montesquieu has said, "Our duty is, to reverence God, not to avenge him." Let us consider well his words : They do not mean that we are to neglect the maintenance of public decorum; but, as the judicious author of the "Essay on Crimes and Punishments" observes, they demonstrate the absurdity of the attempts of an insect, to avenge the insulted majesty of the arbitrator of the universe. Neither the magistrate of a petty village, nor the judge of an imperial city, is a Moses or a Joshua.

CHAP. VI.

Of the indulgence of the Romans in Matters of Religion.

THROUGHOUT Europe, the conversation of enlightened men has often turned upon the surprising contrast existing between the Roman laws, and the barbarous institutions by which they were succeeded and obscured, as the ruins of a splendid city are hidden by accumulating rubbish.

Doubtless the Roman Senate felt as profound a veneration for the Supreme Being as we do; and held the secondary immortal gods, who were dependent upon their eternal ruler, in as much consideration as we do the saints. *Ab Jove puncipium*, was the common form of invocation. Pliny* in his panegyric on Trajan, begins by averring, that the Romans never omitted to invoke the Deity when they entered upon business, or at the commencement of their speeches. Cicero and Livy confirm the assertion: No people were ever more religious; bu they were also too wise, and too magnanimous to condescend to

* Bene ac sapienter patres conscripti majores instituerunt ut rerum agendarum ita dicendi initium a precationibus cepere, &c.

punish idle language, or philosophical opinions. They were incapable of inflicting a barbarous punishment on those, who, with Cicero, himself an augur, had no faith in auguries; still less did they persecute those, (and among others Julius Cæsar, who made the assertion before the assembled senate,) who said, that the gods do not punish men after death.

It has been often remarked, that the senate permitted the chorus in the Troades, to utter the following sentiments before the audience, in the public theatre at Rome.

" There is nothing to be looked for after death, and death itself is nothing. Thou askest, in what place the dead remain?—where they remained before they had existence."

If there ever was profanity, surely this is it; and, from Ennius to Ausonius, all is profanity, notwithstanding the respect generally paid to public worship. Why were these things disregarded by the Roman senate? Simply because they did not interfere with the government of the state; and did no injury whatever to any institution, or religious ceremony. The *police* of the Romans was, excellent; and, notwithstanding what we have just related, they continued to be absolute masters of the fairest portion of the world till the reign of Theodosius the second.

The maxim of the senate was, *Deorum offensæ Diis curæ :*—that offences committed against the gods concerned the gods alone. The senators themselves being at the head of religious affairs, were under no apprehensions that they might be forced by a convocation of priests to administer to *their* vengeance, under the pretext that the Almighty was to be avenged. They never said, "let us tear the impious to pieces, lest we be deemed impious ourselves—let us prove to the priesthood by our cruelty, that we are not less religious than they."

Yes—but *our* religion is more holy than that of the Romans—Impiety is, therefore, a much greater crime with us than with them : granted—God will punish it ;—the duty of man, is to punish the criminality of impiety when it assumes the shape of public disorder. But, if, in committing the act of impiety, not even a handkerchief has been stolen by the offender; if he has not done the smallest injury to any one ; if the rites of religion have not been disturbed ; shall we punish (I repeat) the man committing such an act of impiety as we would a parricide? The Marechale d'Ancre caused a white cock to be killed at the full of the Moon—Does such an act of folly call upon us to burn alive the Marechale d'Ancre?

> Est modus in rebus, sunt certi denique fines.
> Nec scutica dignum horribili sectare flagello.

CHAP. VII.

Of the crime of unlawful preaching. Story of Anthony.

A CALVANIST preacher, if he comes secretly into certain of the provinces for the purpose of preaching clandestinely to a congregation, is punished with death, if discovered; and those who may have furnished him with a meal, or a nights lodging, are liable to be sent to the galleys for life.

In some countries, a Jesuit detected preaching, is hanged. Is it for the purpose of revenging God's cause, that the Calvanist and Jesuit are ordered to be executed? Do not both parties justify their deeds by the following evangelical law; *Whosoever hearkeneth not unto the church, let him be treated as a heathen and a publican?* But the gospel does not enjoin us to hang either the heathen or the publican.

Or have they built upon the passage in Deuteronomy*—*If among you a prophet arise, and that which he saith come to pass, and he saith unto you, Let us follow strange gods; and if thy brother, or thy son, or thy wife, or the friend of thy heart, say unto thee, come let us follow strange gods: let them straightway be killed; strike thou first, and all the people after thee?*—But neither the Calvinist nor the Jesuit have said:—*Come let us follow strange gods.*

The Counsellor *Dubourg*, the canon *Jehan Chauvin*, commonly called *Calvin*, the Spanish physician *Servetus*, and *Gentilis*, a native of Calabria, all worshipped the same God; yet the President *Minard* caused Dubourg to be hanged, and the friends of Dubourg procured the assassination of Minard. Calvin caused Servetus to be burned alive; and had the additional consolation of successfully contributing, in no ordinary degree, to bring Gentilis to the block: the successors of Calvin burned Anthony. Was it reason, piety, or justice that produced all these murders?

* Chap. xiii.

The story of Anthony is one of the most singular we find recorded in the annals of Frenzy. The following account of him I have extracted from a very curious manuscript; and the story is also partly related by Jacob Spohn.

Anthony was born at Brieu in Lorraine, of Catholic parents, and studied at Pont-a-Mousson with the Jesuits. At Metz he was converted to the protestant faith by the preacher Feri. On his arrival at Nancy, he was prosecuted as a heretic; and, but for the timely assistance of a friend, would inevitably have been hanged. He fled for refuge to Sedan, where, being taken for a papist, he narrowly escaped assassination.

As if aware that same strange fatality attended him, and convinced that his life was safe neither among protestants nor catholics, he went to Venice, and there embraced Judaism. He was sincere in the persuasion, and maintained it, too, to the last moment of his life, that the Jewish was the only true religion; and, that as it had once been so, it would forever continue so to remain. His Jewish brethren did not circumcise him, for fear of giving offence to the civil magistrate; but he was not, on that account, the less a Jew at heart. He made no open profession of his new

A a

faith; and having taken a journey to Geneva, in the character of a preacher, he became president of the college, and finally exercised the office that there gives the title of *Minister*.

The continual combat in his breast, between the doctrine of Calvin, which he was under the necessity of preaching, and the religion of Moses, the only religion in which he believed, produced a long illness. He became melancholy, and finally quite deranged; in his agonies he exclaimed, that he was a Jew. The ministers of the gospel came to visit, and endeavoured to bring him back to reason; but he answered, "That he adored none but the God of Israel; that it was impossible for God to change; and that God could never have promulgated, engraven with his own hand, a law he purposed to abolish." He declaimed against Christianity, but afterwards retracted all that he had said; he wrote a profession of Faith, for the purpose of escaping punishment; but, after having written it, the unfortunate persuasion of his heart prevented him from signing it; and the city council assembled to ascertain what was to be done with the unhappy man. The minority of the priests, assembled for this purpose, were of opinion, that he was an object of compassion; and that their first endeavours should be directed to cure his mental disorder, rather than to inflict punishment on him. The majority, however, decided that he deserved to be burned alive, which was accordingly executed. This transaction took place in 1632.* A century of reason and virtue scarcely suffice to expiate such a deed.

CHAP. VIII.

The Story of Simon Morin.

THE tragical end of Simon Morin is hardly less shocking than that of Anthony. In the midst of the gaieties of a splendid court, surrounded by gallantry and pleasure, and during the season of greatest festivity at Paris this unhappy wretch breathed his last in the flames, in the year 1663. He was a deranged man, who believed that he saw visions; and even carried his folly so far as to imagine, that he was sent from God, and gave out that he was incorporated with Jesus Christ.

The parliament, very judiciously, condemned him to imprisonment in a mad-house. What is exceeding singular, there was, at that time, confined in the same mad-house, another crazy

* Jacob Spohn, page 500. and Guy Vances.

of a Prophet. He pretended that God had placed in his hands, the key of the treasures of the Apocalypse; that with that key he would produce the reform of all human kind; and that he was about to march against the Jansenists with an army of an hundred and forty thousand men.

Nothing could have been more rational than to have confined him in the same cell with Simon Morin: will it be credited that he met with encouragement from the Jesuit *Annat*, the king's confessor? He persuaded Annat, that poor Simon Morin was establishing a sect almost as dangerous as Jansenism itself; and, finally, having carried his infamy so far as to turn informer, he obtained from the *Lieutenant-criminel*, an order for the arrest of his unfortunate rival. I scarce dare relate the result—Simon Morin was condemned to be burned alive.

When about to conduct him to the stake, the executioner found a paper in one of his stockings in which he begged forgiveness of God for all his errors—that alone ought to have saved him, but the sentence was irrevocable, and he was executed without mercy.

Such deeds harrow up the soul—yet shew me

the country, where scenes as dreadful have not taken place? Men have every where forgotten that they were brethren, and have persecuted each other " even unto death." The most powerful consolation to human nature is, that those dreadful times are past away, to return no more.

CHAP. IX

Of Witches.

IN 1749, a woman was burned in the Bishopric of Wurtzburg, for the crime of witchcraft—An extraordinary phenomenon in the present century. Is it possible that nations who boast of their reformation; of trampling superstition under foot; who, indeed, supposed that they had attained the perfection of reason, could believe in witchcraft; and, upon the strength of such belief, proceed to burn poor women accused of that crime, and this, more than an hundred years after the pretended reformation of their reason?

About the year 1652, a country-woman, named *Michelle Chaudron*, belonging to the little territory of Geneva, met the Devil, in the road leading out of the city. The Devil gave her a kiss, received her homage, and imprinted on her upper lip, and right breast, the mark he is wont to bestow on those whom he chooses to distinguish as favorites. This seal of the Devil, is a little mark, which renders the skin insensible, as we are assured by the demonographical civilians of those times.

The Devil then ordered Michelle Chaudron to bewitch two girls. She obeyed her master punctually. The parents of the girls took legal measures against her for the crime of witchcraft. The girls were interrogated, and confronted with the accused. They declared that they felt a continual pricking all over their bodies, and that they were bewitched. Physicians, at least those who were called physicians at that time, were called in. They examined the girls. They also searched on the body of Michelle for the devil's marks, called in the statement of the case, *satanic marks*. Into one of these, they thrust a long needle, which produced no trifling degree of torture. The blood flowed readily enough; and Michelle gave sufficient evidence by her cries, that the *satanic marks* had not rendered the part insensible. The judges finding the evidence of Michelle's being a witch, defective, proceeded to torture her; a method that infallibly furnishes sufficient evidence of any fact: the wretched woman confessed during her agonies, every thing they desired.

The physicians again sought the satanic marks. They found a little black spot upon one of her thighs. Into this they thrust the needle. The torture the poor creature had undergone rendered her insensible to the pain, and she did not cry out; of course, the crime was fully proved. But as a dawn of civilization then began to appear in the world, she was strangled previous to being burned. At the period of which we are speaking, (1652.) every tribunal of christian Europe resounded with similar sentences; and fire and faggot were universally employed, as well against witchcraft as heresy. Nay, it was thought a matter of reproach to the Turks, that they had neither witches nor demoniacs among them; and, the absence of the latter, was urged as a decisive proof of the falsehood of their religion.

A zealous friend to public welfare, humanity and true religion, has, in one of his works in favor of innocence, informed us, that christian tribunals have condemned to death, above an hundred thousand persons accused of the crime of witchcraft. If to these judicial murders be added the much superior number of immolated heretics, that portion of the globe will be found to resemble a vast scaffold, covered with victims and executioners, and surrounded by judges, guards and spectators.

CHAP. X.

Of capital punishment.

IT is an old observation, that a man, after he is hanged, is good for nothing; and that punishments intended to benefit society, should, at the same time, be useful to society. It is very evident, that a score of robust highway men, condemned for life to labour on some public work, render through the medium of their punishment, some service to the state; and that their deaths would be of service to no one but the public executioner. Thieves are seldom executed in England; transportation to the colonies is substituted. A similar plan was pursued throughout the vast empire of Russia, where the self-created power of Elizabeth, during its whole continuance, did not require a single execution. The superior genius who succeeded her,† Catherine 2d, has adopted the same maxim.

† In 1762.

It has not been discovered that crimes multiply in consequence of this humanity; and generally speaking, criminals banished to Siberia have been thoroughly reformed. The same remark has been made with regard to the English colonies. This happy change astonishes us—yet nothing is more natural. The convicts are obliged to labour incessantly in order to support life; opportunities for vice are wanting; they marry, and a new population is the consequence. Oblige men to labor, and you render them respectable. It is notorious that few crimes of an atrocious cast, are committed in the country, except, perhaps, when too many holidays lead to idleness and consequent debauchery.

A Roman citizen was never capitally punished, except for crimes that endangered the safety of the republic. They, our masters, our first legislators, were sparing of the blood of their fellow-citizens; we are prodigal of that of our own.

The delicate and fatal question, whether a judge is authorised to pronounce sentence of death, when the law does not expressly point out the punishment of a crime, has often been discussed. It was solemnly argued before the Emperor Henry 7th.* who decided, that no judge could exercise such a power.

There are, certainly, some criminal cases, either so rare, so complicated, or attended by such extraordinary circumstances, that the laws of more than one country have been obliged to leave the remedies for such singular occurrences to be determined by the discretion of judges.

But where there happens *one case*, in which it becomes necessary to put to death a criminal to whom the law does not adjudge death as the measure of his punishment, a thousand cases arise, in which humanity would lead us to spare life, in opposition to the sentence of the law.†

The sword of Justice is committed to our hands; but, we ought rather to blunt, than ren-

---

* Bodin, *de Republica*, lib. 3. chap v.

† Infinitely less mischief arises from suffering a crime to go unpunished, than to sentence the criminal to capital punishment when unauthorised by an express provision of law. It is depriving punishment of its legitimate character, that of being inflicted as a consequence of crime, and not as avenging the guilt of any particular individual. Any law permitting a judge to inflict the punishment of death, secures impunity to him should he exercise the power; but it cannot absolve him from the guilt, (in a moral point of view) of murder. Besides, how is it possible to conceive the existence of a crime, as detrimental to the welfare of society as the continuance in being of the man who commits would be dangerous, and yet that the occurrence of this very crime should never be anticipated by an enlightened legislator; that it should be as well difficult to foresee, as to determine with precision the acts by which it shall be constituted?

der its edge more keen:' It remains in its sheath in the presence of royalty—'tis to admonish us that it should be rarely drawn.

In addition to these reflections, we should not forget, that there have been Judges who delighted in blood; such was Jeffreys, in England; such, in France, was the character who received the surname of *Coup-tête*.* Those men were never born to the magistracy; nature intended them for the executioners of Justice.

CHAP. XI.

Of the Execution of Sentences.

MUST we go to the extremities of the earth, must we have recourse to the law of China, to learn how sparing we ough: to be of human blood? The tribunals of that country have existed during a period of more than four thousand years; yet, at the present day, a peasant, at the extremity of the empire, remains unexecuted, until the proceedings in his case have been transmitted to the emperor, who causes them to be thrice reviewed by one of his tribunals;

* The beheader.

after which, he signs the warrant for execution, or commutation of punishment, or grants him a pardon.*

Let us not travel so far for examples, while Europe abounds with them. No criminal is ever executed in England whose death-warrant is unsigned by the king: the same regulation prevails in Germany, and in most countries of the north of Europe. In France, the same custom anciently existed; and always ought to exist in every civilized nation. Cabal, prejudice, and ignorance, may dictate sentences when they are not to be reviewed by the throne; and little local intrigues are unknown to, and disregarded by a court employed as it always is, by objects of importance.

The supreme council of a state consists of men more accustomed to business, and less liable to prejudice; the habit of regarding great affairs only, renders them less presuming, because less ignorant; and they are, of course, more capable

---

* The author of the "*Spirit of Laws*," who has intermingled so many charming truths in his work, seems to be egregiously mistaken, when, in order to support his assertion, that the vague sentiment of honor is the support of monarchies, and virtue of republics, he says of the Chinese: "I am ignorant in what honor consists among nations who are governed by the Bastinado." Surely, because they disperse the mob with a cudgel, and punish rogues and vagabonds with the bamboo, it does not follow, that China is not governed by tribunals that are a mutual check to each other; or, that is not an excellent form of government.—

of judging than the inferior judge of a province, whether the *whole state* requires or not an example of severity in punishment. In short, whenever inferior courts have determined a case according to the strict letter of the law, an interpretation often rigorous, the supreme council mitigates the sentence in obedience to the dictates of general law, which teaches us, never to sacrifice our fellow-creatures, but upon the most evident necessity.

CHAP. XII.

Of Torture.

ALL mankind, being exposed to the attemps of perfidy or violence, detest crimes of which they may possibly be the victims. All unite in the desire of punishing the principal offender and his accomplices; but all, nevertheless, through a sentiment of pity which God has implanted in our hearts, are roused to resist the practice of torturing the accused from whom a confession is wished to be extorted. The law, as yet, has not judged them guilty; and, a punishment is inflicted upon them, while we are in a state of uncertainty as to the crime they are supposed to have committed, more terrible than the death awarded them when we are satisfied as to their guilt. What! 'I am ignorant whether thou art guilty or not, and I must proceed to put thee to the torture in order to satisfy my doubts; and, if thou shouldest be innocent, I will never recompence thee for the thousand deaths I have made thee suffer instead of the one which, at the same time, I was preparing for thee.' Every being shudders at the thought. I shall not here rely upon the fact that St. Augustine, in his *City of God*, has protested against the practice. I will not say that the Romans never tortured any but slaves; and, that Quintilian, recollecting that even slaves were men, revolted at such barbarity.

If there were but one country in the world that had abolished the torture; if there were as few crimes committed in that country as in any other; if, besides, that country were more flourishing since the abolition; the one example is sufficient for the rest of the world. Let England alone instruct other countries, although she stands not alone in this good work; the torture having been abolished with success in some other countries —The question, therefore, is at rest. Shall not nations then who pique themselves on their politeness, pride themselves also upon their humanity?

Will they persist in an inhuman practice, merely because it is the custom of the country? Reserve such cruelty, if it be necessary to reserve it, for those hardened villains who shall have assassinated the head of a family or the father of his country; but do not suffer the blot of inflicting on a youth, for trival faults, the same measure of punishment that you would decree to a parricide, to remain on your country. I am ashamed of having touched upon this subject, after what has been said by the author of the Esssay on Crimes and Punishments—I ought to have rested satisfied with wishing, that mankind would often reperuse the work of that friend to humanity.

CHAP. XIII.

Of certain sanguinary tribunals.

WILL it be believed that there existed formerly a supreme tribunal more horrible than the Inquisition; and that that tribunal was established by Charlemagne? It was the judgment of Westphalia, otherwise called the "*Vhemic Court.*" The severity, or rather, the cruelty of this Court, was carried so far as to punish every Saxon with death, who broke his fast during the continuance of Lent. The same law was also established in Flanders and Franche Comté in the beginning of the seventeenth century.

In the archives of a corner of the country, called St. Claude, situated among the most frightful rocks of the county of Burgundy, are preserved the proceedings sentence, and account of the execution of a poor gentleman, named Claude Guillon, who was beheaded on the twenty-eighth of July 1629. Reduced to great indigence, and prest by extreme hunger, he ate, on a fish day, a morsel of Horse-flesh which he took from the animal which had been killed in a neighbouring field. Such was his crime. He was condemned as a sacrilegious person. If he had been rich, and had spent two hundred crowns in procuring an extravagant fish supper, while at the same time he suffered the poor around him to die with hunger, he would have been looked upon as a man who fulfilled every duty. The following is a copy of the sentence pronounced upon him.

" Having seen all the papers in the cause, and heard the opinions of Doctors learned in the law, we hereby declare the said Claude Guillon duly arraigned and convicted of having carried away part of the flesh of a Horse killed in this town, of having caused the said flesh to be cooked on Saturday the 3d. of March, and of having eaten of the same, &c."

What sort of Doctors must those Doctors of law have been, who gave their opinions? Was it among the Topinambous or among the Hottentots that these transactions happened? The Vhemic Court was much more terrible; commissaries secretly appointed by this tribunal, spread themselves all over Germany, receiving accusations without the knowledge of the accused, who were condemned without being heard; and frequently, when in want of an executioner, the youngest of the judges performed the office, and hanged the criminal himself.*

It was necessary, in order to be safe from the assassinations of this court, to procure letters of exemption, and safe conducts from the Emperors, and these were sometimes ineffectual. This Court of murderers was not entirely broken up till the reign of Maximilian the 1st. it should have been dissolved in the blood of its members. The Venetian Council of Ten was, by comparison with this court, a tribunal of mercy.

* See the excellent abridgment of the Chronological History and Public law of Germany. Ann. 803.

CHAP XIV.

Of the difference between political and natural laws.

I CALL *natural laws*, those which nature has dictated in all ages, and to every people, for the maintenance of the principles of that Justice which nature, notwithstanding all that has been said against it, has implanted in our hearts. Theft, violence, homicide, ingratitude to indulgent parents, perjury committed to injure, not to assist, an innocent person, and conspiracy against our native country, are positive crimes, every where more or less severely, and always justly punished.

I call those, *political laws*, that are made to meet a present emergency, whether for the purpose of strengthening the power of government, or the prevention of future misfortune.

For example; it is apprehended that the enemy may receive intelligence from the inhabitants of a city; you shut the gates immediately, and you forbid any one to pass the ramparts, on pain of death.

Or, when a new sect in religion, making a parade, in public, of its obedience to the sovereign power, cabals in secret for the purpose of throwing off that obedience; and, under the pretext that it is better to obey God than man, and that the reigning sect is loaded with superstition, and ridiculous ceremonies, wishes to destroy that which is deemed sacred by the state, you enact the punishment of death against those, who by dogmatizing publicly in favour of the sect, run the risk of instigating the people to revolt.

Or, two ambitious men are disputing the possession of a throne: the most powerful succeeds; he punishes with death the partisans of his weaker antagonist. Judges become the instrument of the vengeance of the new sovereign, and the supporters of his authority. Whoever had any communication, under Hugh Capet, with Charles of Lorraine, ran the risk of his life unless he was very powerful.

When Richard the third, the murderer of his nephews, was recognized as king of England, a jury condemned Sir William Collinburn to be quartered; his crime was the having written to a friend of the Earl of Richmond, who was at that time raising troops, and who afterwards reigned under the name of Henry the VII : two ridiculous lines of Sir William's writing were found, and they sufficed to consign him to a horrible death. History abounds with similar examples of justice.

The law of retaliation, is also one of those laws the authority of which is admitted by all nations —The enemy has hanged one of your bravest officers, who held out in a little ruined fort against a whole army; one of their officers falls into your hands; he may be an estimable man for whom you may have great regard; yet, you hang him upon the principle of retaliation—You say, it is the law: that is to say, because your enemy has sullied *his* character by one outrageous crime, it becomes necessary for you to commit another.

All those laws, the result of a sanguinary policy, exist but for a time : we easily see that they are not founded on principle, when we observe them to be temporary. They remind us of the necessity which, in cases of extreme famine, obliges men to eat each other : they cease to devour men as soon as bread can be obtained.

CHAP. XV.

Of the crime of High Treason. Of Titus Oates; and of the death of Augustine de Thou.

WE call a blow aimed at the government of our country, or against the sovereign, who represents it, *High treason.* It is looked upon as a species of parricide; and, therefore, the guilt of it ought not to be extended by law to offences which do not bear some analogy to that crime. For if you consider a theft committed in a public building, an act of extortion, or even seditious words, as high treason, you at once lessen the horror, which the crime of high treason, properly so called, ought to inspire.

In the ideas we form of great crimes there should be nothing arbitrary. If a theft committed, or an imprecation uttered against a father, by a son, be considered as parricide, you break the bonds of filial love. The son, in future, will never look upon his father but as an infuriated master. Every thing overstrained in laws tends constantly to their destruction.

In crimes of ordinary occurrence, the laws of England are favourable to the accused; but in the case of high treason, more than unfavorable. The exjesuit Titus Oates, being judicially examined by the house of commons, and, having declared, upon his oath, that he has told the whole truth, subsequently accused the secretary of the duke of York, afterwards James II, and many other persons, of the crime of high treason; and his declarations were received with attention. He at first, swore before the privy council, that he had never seen the secretary and afterwards, that he had seen him. Nothwithstanding the informalities and contradiction accompanying his statement, the secretary was executed.

This same Titus Oates, and another witness, swore, that fifty Jesuits had conspired to assassinate Charles the second; and, that they had seen the commissions, signed by father *Oliva*, general of the Jesuits, for the officers who were to command an army of rebels. The testimony of those two men was considered as sufficient to authorise the tearing out of the hearts of several of those they accused and the dashing them afterwards in their faces. But, seriously speaking ought the testimony of two witnesses to be considered as sufficient to convict any man whom they have a mind to destroy? At least, one would suppose, both ought not to be notorious villains neither ought the facts to which they swear to, be beyond the bounds of possibility.

It is perfectly clear, that if two of the most respectable magistrates of the kingdom, were to accuse any individual of having conspired with the muphti, for the purpose of circumcising the whole council of state, the parliament, the members of the court of exchequer, the archbishop, and the doctors of Sorbonne; it would be in vain for these two magistrates to swear that they had seen the letters of the muphti; every one would suppose that they were both deranged, and that no credit was to be attached to their declaration.—It was quite as extravagant to suppose, that the general of the Jesuits was raising an army in England, as it would be to suppose, that the muphti had sent over for the purpose of attempting to circumcise the court of France. But, unhappily, Titus Oates was believed; that there might remain no species of atrocious folly unthought of by the heart of man.

The laws of England do not consider persons as involved in the guilt of any conspiracy, who may be privy to it, and do not inform: they consider an informer to be as infamous, as the conspirator is guilty. In France, those who are privy to a conspiracy are liable to the punishment of death, if they do not communicate their knowledge. Lewis XI, against whom conspiracies were frequent, made this terrible law; which would never have been thought of by a Lewis XII or a Henry the IV.

⌊This law not only obliges a worthy man to turn informer, and divulge a crime which by proper advice, and firm conduct, he might prevent; but, it exposes him likewise to be punished as a calumniator; nothing being more easy, than for conspirators to take measures to avoid conviction.⌋

This was precisely the case of the truly respectable Augustine de Thou, counsellor of state, and the son of the only good historian of whom France can boast, equal to Guicciardini in understanding, and perhaps superior in point of impartiality. A conspiracy was formed, rather against cardinal Richelieu, than against Lewis XIII: the object of the conspirators was not to betray France to any enemy; for the principal author of the plot was the king's only brother, who certainly did not design to destroy a kingdom to which he was there the heir apparent; there being between him and the throne no one but a dying brother, and two children then in the cradle.

De Thou was culpable neither in the sight of God nor man. One of the agents of *Monsieur*, the king's only brother, of the Duke *de Bouillon*, sovereign prince of Sedan, and of the grand Equerry *d'Effiat Cinq Mars*, had communicated, verbally, the plan of their conspiracy to De Thou, who went immediately to Cinq-Mars, and did his utmost to dissuade him from the enterprise. If he then had informed against the conspiracy, he would have been destitute of the means of establishing the truth of his allegation; he would have been overwhelmed by the denials of the heir apparent of the Crown, of a sovereign prince, and of the king's favourite; as well as by the public execration. He would have exposed himself to the fate of a vile calumniator. The chancellor *Séguier* even admitted the fact I am endeavouring to establish, at the time De Thou was confronted with the grand Equerry. It was during the confrontation, that De Thou, addressing himself to Cinq-Mars, in the following words, which are reported in the statement of the case, said; "*Do you not remember, Sir, that not a day passed over our heads, that I did not mention that business to you, for the purpose of dissuading you from it?*"

Cinq-Mars acknowledged that it was true. De Thou deserved the thanks of his country rather than death: such would have been the decision of the tribunal of human equity. At least he deserved not death from Cardinal Richelieu; but humanity was not Richelieu's virtue. In this particular case, surely, we may observe something stronger than, *summum jus, summa injuria.* The sentence of death of this good man, declares his crime to have been: "*The having a knowledge of, and a participation in, the said conspiracies.*" It does not state also, because he did not inform. Hence it would appear, that to discover that a crime is about to be committed, is to be criminal; and that one merits death, sometimes, for being in possession of eyes and ears.

The least we can say of such a sentence is, that it was not dictated by justice, but was the act of a few commissioners. The *letter* of this murderous law was positive; but, I appeal not only to lawyers, but to all mankind, to say, whether the *spirit* of the law was not perverted?

CHAP. XVI.

Of the revealing of crimes (before commission) by religious confession.

JAURIGNI and Balthazar Gerard, who assassinated the prince of Orange, William I; the dominican Jacques Clement; Chatel Ravaillac, and all the other parricides of those days, confessed themselves before the commission of their crimes. Fanaticism during that deplorable age, was carried to such excess, that confession was but the addition of an inducement to the perpetration of villany : crime became sacred—because, confession was a holy sacrament.

Strada himself says, that " *Jaurigni non ante facinus aggredi sustinuit quam expiatam nexis animam apud dominicanum jacerdotem cælesti pane firmaverit.* Jaurigni dared not undertake that action without having his soul, purged by confession to a dominican friar, fortified by the holy bread."

It appears from the answers to the interrogatoties put to Ravaillac, that this wretch, on quitting the order of the *Feuillants*, and wishing to enter that of the Jesuits, addressed himself to the Jesuit D'Aubigni; and, after giving him an account of several visions that he had seen, shewed him a knife, on the blade of which a heart and a cross were engraven; and said to him: *This heart signifies, that the heart of the king ought to be moved to make war upon the Hugenots.* Perhaps if D'Aubigni had had zeal and prudence enough to have informed the king of those words, and had described the man who uttered them, the best of kings might have escaped assassination.

On the twentieth day of August, 1610, three months after the death of Henry IV, while the hearts of all Frenchmen were yet bleeding, the attorney general *St. Servin*, of still illustrious memory, moved that all Jesuits should be required to sign the four following articles:

1. That the council is superior to the pope.

2. That the pope cannot deprive the king of any of his rights, by excommunication.

3. That ecclesiastics are as completely subject to the king, as other persons.

4. That any priest who is apprised, by confession, of the existence of a conspiracy against the king or state, is bound to give notice of it to the civil magistrate.

On the 22d. of the same month, the parliament published a decree, forbidding Jesuits to undertake the instruction of youth without signing the foregoing four articles: but the court of Rome was at that time so powerful, and that of France so weak, that the decree was entirely disregarded.

One fact is also worthy of remark while noticing the subject of confession, which is, that this very court of Rome which when the life of a sovereign was in question, was unwilling that confessors should divulge what was revealed in confession, yet obliged them to reveal to the inquisition, the names of those priests whom females should accuse in confession of having seduced, or attempted to seduce them. Paul IV, Pius IV, Clement VIII, and Gregory XV required such communications. This was a very dangerous snare for confessors and their penitents. It was turning a sacrament into a register of accusations, and even required sacrilege; for, by the ancient canons, particularly those of the lateran council held under Innocent III, any priest divulging of confession of any nature whatsoever, was liable to be degraded and imprisoned for life. Thus we find four different popes, in the sixteenth and seventeenth centuries, who order a sin of impurity to be divulged, and yet do not permit the crime of parricide to be revealed. A woman, confessing herself to a carmelite friar, acknowledges or feigns, that a cordelier has seduced her; the carmelite is bound to inform against the cordelier. But, let a fanatical assassin, who believes he shall serve God by murdering his king, consult his confessor upon this very case of conscience;—the confessor is guilty of sacrilege, if he interpose to save the life of his sovereign.

This absurd yet horrible contradiction, is one of the unhappy consequences of that continual opposition, which has subsisted for so many ages between ecclesiastical and municipal laws. The citizen found himself entangled on many occasions, either in the crime of sacrilege or that of high treason; and the distinctions of right and wrong were buried in a chaos, from which they have not yet emerged.

The confession of sins has been authorised, in every age, by the practice of almost every nation. The ancients accused themselves during the performance of the misteries of Orpheus, of Isis, of Ceres, and those of the island of Samothracia.— The Jews confessed their sins on the day of solemn expiation, and continue the practice to this day. A penitent selects his confessor, who becomes a penitent in turn; and each of them alternately receives thirty lashes with a whip while reciting the formula of confession, consisting of thirteen words, the sense of which consequently must be general.

None of these confessions were ever other than general; and, of course, could never serve as pretexts for those secret consultations, so often made use of by fanatical penitents for the purpose of sinning with impunity—a pernicious corruption of a salutary institution. Confession, the greatest check to crime, became, in times of confusion and licentiousness, an incentive to wickedness; and, it is more than probable, that for this reason, so many christian communities have abolished a holy institution, which could not but appear to them as dangerous as it was useful.

CHAP. XVII.

Of Counterfeiting money.

THE crime of counterfeiting the coin of a country, is deemed, and justly too, high treason in the second degree: to rob all the individuals of a state, is to betray the state itself. But the question may be asked, whether a merchant, who imports ingots from South America, and converts them into *good money,* be guilty of high treason! and merit death? In almost every country, death is the punishment provided for this crime—yet, he has robbed no one: on the contrary, he has increased the circulation of specie, and done the state a service. But he has arrogated to himself the right of his sovereign; he robs him, in taking to himself the small profit that the king receives upon the coinage. *He* has indeed coined good money; but his example holds out a temptation to others to coin bad. Still, death is a severe punishment for his crime. I once knew a lawyer, who wished such criminals, as useful and ingenious hands, to be condemned to work in the royal mint, with fetters on their legs,

CHAP. XVIII.

Of domestic theft.

IN some countries a trifling domestic theft is punished with death. Is not, I ask, this disportionate punishment, as well dangerous to society, as a temptation to cammit larceny? Let a master prosecute his servant for a theft of a small amount; upon the execution of the unhappy wretch, society regards the master with horror: they then feel, that nature and such laws are at variance, and consequently the law will be, in future, unexecuted.

What then is the result? Masters who are robbed, unwilling to encounter *public opprobrium*, content themselves with discharging a dishonest servant, he steals from some one else, and finally, becomes familiar with iniquity. The punishment of death being the consequence of a considerable robbery, as well as of a trifling theft; he will naturally steal to as great an amount as possible; and, at last, will not hesitate at the commission of murder in order to escape detection.

But, if the punishment is proportioned to the crime; if the domestic guilty of theft be condemned to labor on the public works; then, a master would not hesitate about his conviction, because the public feeling would not stand in his way; and theft would be less frequent. Experience furnishes the lesson, that rigorous laws are productive of crime.

CHAP. XIX.

Of Suicide.

THE celebrated *Du Verger de Haurane*, Abbot of St. Cyran, and generally considered as the founder of Port-Royal, wrote, about the year 1608, a treatise upon Suicide, now become one of the scarcest books in Europe.

" The decalogue, says he, orders us not to kill. Self murder seems to be included in the precept as well as the murder of our neighbour: therefore, if situations occur, in which it is lawful to kill our neighbour, others may occur, in which suicide becomes lawful."

" No one ought however, to attempt his own

life, without first consulting his reason. Public authority, which represents God, may dispose of our lives. Human reason, being a ray of the eternal light, may also represent the reason of God."

St. Cyran extends this argument, which, after all, is but a sophism, to a great length. However, I must confess, that when he descends to particular instances in support of it, he is not easily answered. " A man says he, may kill himself for the service of his prince; for the good of his country; for the advantage of his family."

It does appear that we could with justice refuse our approbation to a *Codrus* or a *Curtius*. What prince would dare to punish the family of a man who devoted himself for his service ?—Nay, there is no soveseign who would dare to leave them unrewarded. St. Thomas said the same thing before the time of St. Cyran. But it is not necessary to have recourse to St. Thomas, to St. Bonaventure, or Haurane, to feel, that a man who dies for his country is entitled to our highest commendation.

St. Cyran concludes, that that which it is praiseworthy to do for others, it is lawful to do to ourselves. The arguments of Plutarch, of Seneca, and of Montaigne, on this subject, are well known, as are those of an hundred other philosophers who have written in favor of suicide. The subject has been exhausted. I do not here propose to defend an action which the law prohibits; but neither the old nor new testament forbid a man to shake off life, when it becomes insupportable. The Roman laws did not forbid self murder. On the contrary, a law of Marcus Antoninus, which was never repealed, provides: " If your father, or your brother, unconvicted of any crime, shall, from pain, through weariness of life, in despair, or from madness, put an end to his life, his will shall nevertheless be deemed valid; or if he dies intestate, his heirs inherit according to law." *

Notwithstanding that humane law of our ancient masters, we draw upon a hurdle, and pierce with a stake, the body of the man who dies a voluntary death; and, at the same time, we render his memory infamous. We dishonor his family as far as lies in our power. We punish the son, because he has lost his father; and the widow, because she is deprived of her husband. We even confiscate the property of the deceased; which is, in fact, tearing from the living a patrimony which belongs to them. This custom, like many others, is derived from our canon law;

* Cod. 1. *De bonis eorum qui sibi mortem, &c. Leg.* 3. §. cod.

v. which deprives of the rites of burial, those who commit suicide: The conclusion drawn from this fact, is, that no one can inherit on earth the property of a man, who is deemed to have forfeited an inheritance in heaven. The canon law, under the head, *de pænitentia*, assures us, that Judas committed a greater sin in hanging himself, than when he betrayed our Saviour.

CHAP. XX.

Of a certain species of mutilation.

WE find in the digest, a certain law of the emperor Adrian† which decrees death as the punishment of physicians who should make eunuchs, either by castration, or by bruising the testicles. The possessions of those who procured themselves to be castrated, were also confiscated by this law. Origen might have been punished under this law, for having submitted to the operation, in consequence of a too literal interpretation of the passage of St. Mathew: " *There be eunuchs, which have made themselves eunuchs for the kingdom of Heaven.*

† *Ad legem Corneliam de sicariis.*

The face of things was changed under succeeding Emperors, who adopted the Asiatic luxury, particularly in the lower empire; at Constantinople eunuchs became Patriarchs, and even commanded the armies of the empire.

In our own times, it is the custom, at Rome, to castrate children in order to render them worthy of being musicians to the Pope; so that *castrato* and *musico del papa*, now are synonimous. Not long since, signs were to be seen at Naples, over the doors of certain barbers, on which were written in large letters *Qui si castrano marivigliosamente i putti*—Boys castrated here in the very best manner.

CHAP XXI.

Of the confiscation consequent upon all the crimes which have been mentioned,

IT is a received maxim of the bar, that, *he who forfeits life, forfeits his effects*—a maxim in greatest rigor in countries where custom holds the place of principle. Thus, as we already have remarked, the children of those who voluntarily terminate their wretched days are doomed to perish with hunger, as if they were the children of a murderer. So that, in every case, an entire family is punished for the crime of an individual.

Thus the father of a family having been sentenced to the galleys for life, in an arbitrary manner, either for having illegally harbored a preacher*, or having heard a sermon preached in a cavern or solitary place, the wife and children are reduced to beggary. That system of Jurisprudence which consists in taking the bread out of the mouths of orphans, and in giving to one man the property of another, was unknown during

* See the edict of may 14th. 1724, published at the sollicitation, and under the inspection of Cardinal Richelieu.

the whole period of the existence of the Roman republic. Sylla first introduced it with his proscriptions, and his example, one would think, ought scarcely to authorise the practice. And, indeed, this system which seems to have been dictated by avarice and inhumanity, was not enforced by Cæsar, by Trajan, nor by the Antonines whose names are still pronounced with respect by every civilized nation. Under Justinian, confiscation took place only in cases of high treason.

It would seem that during the times of feudal anarchy, princes, and feudal lords, not being very rich, endeavored to augment their possessions by the conviction of their subjects, and intended to furnish themselves with a revenue to arise out of crime. Law being, with them, entirely arbitrary, and the Roman Jurisprudence unknown, cruel and ridiculous customs prevailed. But, in modern times the power kings is founded upon immense and certain revenues, and their treasures do not require to be increased by the miserable remains of the fortune of an unfortunate family which are ceded, generally speaking, to the first one who requests them—Should one citizen be permitted to fatten on the blood of another?

In the provinces of France where the Roman

law is established, confiscation does not exist, except within the jurisdiction of the parliament of Thoulouse. It does not prevail in some of the provinces where the customary or unwritten feudal law† is in force as, for example, in the Bourbonnais, the provinces of Berri, Maine, Poitou, and Bretagne, or, at least, real estate is exempted. It was established at Calais formerly, but the English abolished the custom when they were in possession of the place. It is a surprising fact, that the inhabitants of the capital live under a much more rigorous code of laws, than the small cities; so true is it, that a system of jurisprudence is often established by fortuitous circumstances, without regularity, without uniformity, like the cottages in a village.

Who would believe that in the year 1673, that brilliant æra of France, the Attorney general *Omer Talon*, would have expressed himself, in full parliament, on the subject of a young lady named *Canillac*, in the following manner? ‡

" In the XIII of Deuteronomy, God says: If thou comest into a city where idolatary reigneth, thou shalt surely smite the inhabitants of that city

---

† See Butler's Horæ Juridicæ. Phil. edit. page 88.
‡ *Journal du Palais*, Vol. 1. pag. 444.

with the edge of the sword, destroying it utterly, and all that is therein. And thou shalt gather all the spoil thereof into the midst of the street, and shalt burn with fire the city, and all the spoil thereof, for the Lord thy God; and it shall be an heap forever; and there shall cleave nought of the cursed thing unto thine hand."

" In like manner, in the crime of high treason, the children were deprived of their inheritance, which became forfeited to the king. *Naboth* being prosecuted, *quia maledixerat regi*, king *Ahab* took possession of his effects. *David*, being informed that *Mephibosheth* had rebelled, gave all his possessions to *Ziba*, who brought him the news: *Tua sint omnia que fuerunt Mephibosheth.*"

The question to be determined was, who should inherit the paternal estate of Mademoiselle de Canillac; an estate formerly forfeited by her father, ceded by the king to a lord of the treasury, and by him granted to the testatrix. In this cause, relating solely to the possessions of a native of Auvergne, a French attorney general quoted the example of Ahab, king of a part of Palestine, who confiscated the vine of Naboth, after assassinating the owner with the sword of justice; an action become even proverbial for its turpitude, and the application of which is intended to inspire mankind with a horror of usurpation. Surely, the story of the vine of Naboth bore no analogy to the question about the property of Mademoiselle de Canillac. The murder of Mephibosheth the grandson of Saul, and son of Jonathan, the friend and protector of David, and the confiscation of his goods, had not the least affinity with the will of that lady.

With this sort of pedantry, with this folly of quoting matters foreign to the subject, with such ignorance of the first principles of human nature, with such prejudices ill conceived, and worse applied, has jurisprudence been commented on by men who have enjoyed reputation in their profession. I leave it to my readers to supply reflections it would be superfluous to insert.

CHAP. XXII.

Of criminal proceedings, and of some other forms of procedure.

IF it should ever happen in France, that some of our too rigorous customs be softened by the laws of humanity, without, however, affording greater facility to crime, I am inclined to think that a reformation will take place in those proceedings, in the enactment of which our legislators appear to have been influenced by too rigid a zeal. Our criminal law, in many respects, seems directed entirely to the destruction of the accused. It is the only uniform system of law in the whole kingdom, and it ought to be as terrible to the guilty, as favorable to the innocent. In England, mere false imprisonment, is a ground for recovering damages from the first minister of state, if he orders it; but, in France, an innocent man who has been immured in a dungeon, who has undergone the torture, has no consolation of that kind to hope for, no one to look to for damages; and he returns to society with a ruined reputation. Why? Because his joints have been dislocated—*that*, should excite pity, and inspire respect. The discovery of crimes, it is said, requires severity: it is the war of human justice against iniquity—But, even in a state of war, there is something like generosity and compassion. The soldier is compassionate—Shall the lawgiver alone encourage the exercise of barbarity?

Let us here compare the Roman method of conducting criminal proceedings with our own. With them, the witnesses were publicly examined in the presence of the accused, who had the privilege of cross-examining them, either by himself or his counsel. This method of proceeding was frank and noble; it was full of Roman magnanimity.

With us, every thing is transacted in secret. A single judge, attended only by his clerk, hears all the witnesses, who are examined separately. This method, established by Francis 1st. was confirmed by the commissioners appointed to arrange and modify the ordinances of Lewis-XIV. 1670; its confirmation was owing to a mistake. They took it into their heads in reading the code *de Testibus*, that the words, *testes intrare judicii secretum*,* meant, that witnesses were examined in

---

* See *Bornier*, Tit VI, art. II. *des informations*.

private; but *secretum* here means the Judge's chamber. *Intrare secretum*, if intended to signify private examination, would not be Latin. A solecism was the foundation of this part of our Jurisprudence.

The witnesses, in criminal cases, are generally the dregs of the populace, whom the Judge, during private examination, may make say whatever he pleases. These witnesses are examined a second time, but still privately; and, if, upon their second examination, they retract what they said during the first, or vary in essential circumstances, they are proceeded against for perjury. So that when a simple but honest man unable to express himself with clearness, but with every disposition to tell the truth, recollecting that he has said too much, or too little, that he has misunderstood the judge, or that the judge has misunderstood him, retracts what he has said, from a principle of justice, he is punished as a villian. He is forced to adhere to false testimony to avoid the consequences of perjury.

The accused, if he flies, exposes himself to certain conviction; and this whether his crime be clearly proved or not. Some writers on Jurisprudence, indeed, have maintained, that contumacy ought not alone to be a sufficient ground for conviction; but, that the charge ought to be fully proved. But others, less enlightened, though, perhaps, more generally followed, are of the contrary opinion: they advance the doctrine, that the flight of the accused is full proof of his crime—that the contempt exhibited by him for justice, in refusing to appear, deserves the same degree of punishment that would follow a solemn conviction. Thus it depends, upon the sect of lawyers to which the judge may happen to belong whether an innocent man be convicted or acquitted.

One other great abuse also prevalent in French Jurisprudence is, that the reveries, and errors, sometimes having the cruellest tendency, of abandoned men, who have undertaken to give publicity to their sentiments on legal matters, are considered as law.

Two ordinances, during the reign of Lewis the 14th, were promulgated, which are in force throughout the kingdom. In the first, which relates entirely to civil proceedings, the judges are forbidden to give judgment, in a civil suit, by default, if the demand is not proved; but in the second, regulating criminal cases, contains no provision that the accused, if no evidence be produced against him, shall be discharged. Extraordinary fact! The law provides that he from whom a trifling sum of money is demanded, shall not be adjudged to pay it without the debt is established—but when life is in question, it is a *moot* point, whether he ought not to be convicted if contumacious, although the crime be not proved.

Suppose the accused withdraws himself from justice: you proceed to seize and take an inventory of his property: you do not even wait until the proceeding is finished. You have as yet no evidence of his crime: you do not know whether he is innocent or guilty; and you commence proceedings by forcing upon the defendant immense unnecessary expense.

It is the penalty, you say, of his disobedience to the warrant issued against him—But, I ask, is not the extreme rigor of your criminal practice, the cause of his disobedience? A man is accused of a crime, you proceed to immure him immediately in a frightful dungeon; you suffer no one to have communication with him; he is loaded with fetters, as if already convicted. The witnesses who testify against him are examined in secret, and in his absence. He sees them only for a moment at the confrontation; and then, before he has heard their testimony, he is bound immediately to stase his objections to the witnesses, and at the same time, to name the witnesses in support of those objections; and he has not the right to crossexamine them after the reading of their testimony. If, however, he should convince the witnesses, that they may have exaggerated some facts, omitted others, or have been mistaken in some of the particulars they have related, the fear of punishment will induce them to persist in perjury. And, if circumstances admitted by the accused when interrogated, be differently related by the witnesses, that alone will be sufficient grounds for ignorant or prejudiced judges to condemn an innocent man.

What man is there that such a proceeding would not terrify? Where is the innocent man who can be sure of acquittal? O judges! are you desirous that the accused should not fly?—Furnish him with the means of defence.

The law seems to oblige the magistrate to conduct himself towards a prisoner, rather as his enemy, than as his judge. This judge, however, possesses the power of confronting the accused with the witnesses, or omitting it altogether*.—Why is so essential a thing as confrontation suffered to be optional?

* *Et si besoin est confrontez*, (And, if necessary, confront them.) says the Ordinance of 1670. art. 1. tit. XV.

The practice adopted, however, is, in this respect, contrary to a law which is equivocal; there is always a confrontation; but the judge does not always confront all the witnesses, he omits often those whose statements appear to him to be unimportant. Such a witness, though he say nothing against a man in the body of his testimony, may, upon confrontation, testify in his favor. The witnesess also may have forgotten circumstances favorable to the accused; the judge at first may not have felt the weight of those circumstances, and may not have reduced them to writing. It is, therefore, extremely important that *all* the witnesses should be confronted with the accused, and that such confrontation be not optional with the judge.

When it is a criminal charge, the accused cannot have the benefit of counsel to defend him; he flies—a step to which every maxim of law incites him—But, he may be convicted in his absence, whether the crime with which he is charged be proved or not. Strange doctrine! If a civil suit to recover a sum of money be brought against a man, a judgment by default cannot be obtained without proof of the debt—yet, if a matter involving his life occur, he may be sentenced in his absence, without a necessity for a shadow of evidence to substantiate his crime. The law then holds money in more estimation that it does life? O ye Judges! consult the pious Antoninus, and the good Trajan—they suffered not the absent to be condemned. †

Your laws allow an extortioner, or a fraudulent bankrupt the benefit of counsel, and very often deny it to one who may be an honest man. If there can be shewn one single case, where innocence has been made to triumph through the exertions of an advocate, the injustice of depriving any one of the advantage is manifest.

The president *Lamoignon* said, in speaking against this law, " that the advocate, or counsel, which it was the practice to assign to the accused, was not a privilege granted by the ordinances, nor by the laws of the kingdom—it was a privilege derived from the law of nature, a law more ancient than any human institution. Nature, said he, points out to every man the necessity of having recourse to the talents of others, when he finds himself in a situation where they are indispensible to his safe guidance, and he feels that he cannot conduct himself; he seeks assistance when un-

† Dig. 1. 1. tit. *de absertibus*, and l. 5. tit. *de pœnis*.

able to defend himself with his own strength. Our ordinances have taken away from accused persons so many advantages, that the least we can do, in justice, is to preserve those few that remain to them, inviolate; and most particularly the benefit of counsel. And, if our proceedings be compared with those of the Romans, and other nations, it will be found, that in no nation are they so rigorous, as in France, particularly since the ordinance of 1539. ‡

The proceedings are still more rigorous since the ordinance of 1670. They would have been much less so, if all the commissioners had thought like Monsieur de Lamoignon. The parliament of Thoulouse has a singular degree of accuracy in weighing the testimony of witnesses. In other places demi-proofs are admitted, which is at most admitting doubts, there being no such thing as demi-truth; but at Thoulouse they admit of quarters and eighths of a proof. We may, for example, look upon hearsay, as a quarter, upon another hearsay, more vague still, as an eighth; so that eight rumours, which are but the echo of unfounded report, may become a complete proof; and upon such evidence as this it was, that John Calas was sentenced to the wheel. The Roman law required proofs to be *luce meridiana clariores.*

‡ *Proces verbal de l'ord.* p. 163.

CHAP. XXIII.

The idea of a reform suggested.

THE Magistracy is in itself so respectable, that the only country in the world where the office is venal, sincerely desires a deliverance from the evil resulting from this custom. They anxiously desire to see justice dispensed by the advocate, who has contributed by his industry, by his writings, and by his eloquence to its defence and support. Perhaps we might then see a regular system of Jurisprudence arise, the result of enlightened exertions.

Shall the same cause be forever *decided* one way in the provinces and another in the capital? must the same man be always right in Britanny and wrong in Languedoc? nay, there are as many systems of Jusprudence as there are cities; and in the same parliament the maxims of one chamber are not the maxims of another.

To shew the astonishing contrariety of law in the same kingdom, we have only to state, that in Paris, a man who has been domiciled in the city a year and a day, becomes a citizen. In *Franche-*

Compté, a free man, who, during a year and a day, has inhabited a house held in Mortmain, becomes a slave: his collateral relations cannot inherit the property he may have acquired elsewhere; and his children are deprived of their inheritance, if they have been a year absent from the house in which their father died.

When limits are to be determined between the civil law and the ecclesiastical authority, what endless disputes ensue! Who can point out those limits? Who can reconcile the eternal contradictions of the treasury and the bench? In short, why, in certain countries, do we find sentences which do not state the facts and reasons upon which they are grounded? Are they ashamed to avow their reasons for rendering judgment. And why do not those who condemn in the name of their sovereign, present their sentences of death for reconsideration to him, before they are put in execution!

Look around us where we will, we find nothing but a confused scene of contradiction, hardship, uncertainty, and arbitrary power. Thence arises our desire to render more perfect the laws upon which our lives and fortunes depend.

THE END.

Printed in the United States
121949LV00005B/115-123/A